Ruth Anne,

God bless you

Mary Flynn

ALL WE LIKE SHEEP

ALL WE LIKE SHEEP

MARY GLYNN PEEPLES

P.O. Box 76046 • Birmingham, Alabama 35253 • (205) 871-0380

Unless otherwise identified scripture quotations are from the King James Version of the Bible.

Scripture quotations identified Living Bible are from the Living Bible Version of the Bible copyrighted 1971 and 1973.

To my three children,
Sam, Dawn and Mark

Contents

Acknowledgments
Author's Note

Acknowledgments

I want to thank my husband, Sam, for his patience and kindness in helping me organize the material in this book. Since he sold his dental practice in 1972, we have worked side by side teaching, speaking, counseling, raising children, eating and sleeping! He is my teacher and my counselor. He has been an example to me of a man who walks with the Lord in control of his life. I have been able to recommend his lifestyle to our sons and our son-in-law. I thank God for giving Sam to me as a partner for life.

I want to express to Dr. Henry Brandt my deep appreciation for his counsel. He has never failed to give me advice based on the Bible. At times I have not wanted to hear the truth but this never caused Henry to back away from speaking it. I have had many problems and needed solutions. Henry has faithfully guided my thinking according to the Word of God. Thank you, Henry.

Elizabeth Rhodes, thank you for sharing your talent. Your watercolors found in this book have made it fun! Your excitement and enthusiam has spurred me on to complete what I started.

Tim Wilson, thank you for helping me edit the copy. You came along at the perfect time to help with commas, semi-colons, and all those rules I learned but have forgotten!

To you, the reader — I pray that you will be able to identify with my stories and decide that you, like a sheep, need a shepherd. I desire for you to follow my shepherd, Jesus Christ. He is able to supply your needs according to the riches of His glory, to strengthen you by His might, to enable you to know His love which passeth all knowledge and to do exceeding abundantly above all that you ask or think according to His power.

Author's Note

This book, All We Like Sheep, is a practical guide for living the Christian life. You may be wondering about the title! Does it seem strange? Let me help you. These are the first four words from a statement made by the old testament prophet, Isaiah. In the book of Isaiah, chapter 53, verse 6, we read, "All we like sheep have gone astray; we have turned every one to his own way; and the LORD hath laid on Him the iniquity of us all."

Two of the key reasons for my study of the Bible are:
1. To learn what God says about Himself.
2. To learn what God says about me.

Many places in the Bible we find that God likens us to sheep. God created both man and animals. Realizing this, I decided to examine carefully this animal.

For the past 10 years I have been accumulating information about sheep. This also led to an interest in shepherds and their responsibilities. I am excited about what I have learned! In Part I, I have chosen ten characteristics of sheep to share with you. The goal of relating this information: to show our need of following God's provided shepherd, the Lord Jesus Christ.

To best communicate each characteristic I have divided the information into four sections:
1. Characteristics of sheep
2. A shepherd's care
3. Characteristics of people
4. The shepherd's care

Part II describes how we, like sheep, have turned to our own way. The nature of human nature is to want to have our own way. This strong natural tendency can get us in trouble when it overrides what we know to be right. Our reactions when things don't go our way will trouble us.

In Part III, we read the good news! "And the Lord (God) hath laid on Him (Jesus, the Messiah) the iniquity of us all." I believe the word iniquity can best be defined as wanting to have our own way. Herein lies God's provision for our tendency to want to have our way and the reactions when we don't get our way. The provision is in Christ's atoning death, His resurrection and His coming to live in our lives (when we invite Him in). Practical applications are given so you can benefit from God's provision.

I pray that you will be motivated afresh to follow confidently our Lord, The Shepherd.

PART I

All We Like Sheep . . .

The telephone rang in the dead of night. I began to grope for the receiver. Finding it, I managed a weak and husky hello. The voice on the other end of the line said, "Mary Glynn, are you asleep?" I felt that question did not deserve an answer!

Barbara was crying, "Jeff has run away from home." Jeff was Barbara's 16 year old son. He had decided that life was too short to have to live with his parent's rules. He wanted to make his own decisions.

Mary called at eight a.m. "I have to talk to you. I'll pick you up and we will go for a ride. I do not want anyone in your house to hear what I have to say." Mary's son had decided he wanted to do his own thing. It just so happened that "his thing" was not what his parents had in mind for him to do!

Agnes came in the front door sobbing. Her head was buried in her hands. Her husband Joe had done it again. He had promised he would stop seeing Lois. Agnes caught them together the night before.

Alice came by to tell me that her telephone was out of order. We called the number and the nice voice on the recording said that we had reached a number that had been temporarily disconnected. What did the telephone company mean disconnecting her telephone? Surely her husband had paid the bill! He promised he would pay all bills on time this month.

How do you explain such behavior? How do you help these victims handle their reactions and help them decide what they should do about such treatment?

I have had my share of crises and unexpected problems that intruded into my life and I found an answer. I have been sharing my solution

1

in seminars and in counseling. That is why these people called me. I have discovered a "manual" written by the Creator of us all, called the Bible.

This manual says of itself in II Timothy chapter 3 verses 16 and 17: "All scripture is given by inspiration of God, and is profitable for doctrine, for reproof, for correction for instruction in righteousness: That the man of God may be perfect, throughly furnished unto all good works."

All scripture is given by God and is profitable, let's stop here! All people want to live profitable lives. Our Creator has declared to us that which is profitable. In a recent article George Gallop said, "America is truly spiritually illiterate." In a recent survey 8 out of 10 Americans identified themselves as Christians. Yet only 4 out of 10 knew that Jesus Christ delivered the sermon on the mount! If you want to live a profitable life, then you will need to be knowledgeable of the Bible. You need to understand its doctrines in order to know why you believe it to be truth. Reproof is not a pleasant experience but a necessary one. Through reproof, God shows us what needs to be changed and corrected. We learn how to be righteous and that simply means how to choose the correct behavior. The purpose for this exercise is explained in the verse: "we can be furnished unto all good works." It feels good to know you have done the right thing.

This manual again describes itself in Hebrews chapter 4 verse 12: "The Word of God is quick and powerful, and sharper than any twoedged sword, piercing even to the dividing asunder of soul and spirit, and of the joints and marrow, and is a discerner of the thoughts and intents of the heart."

The Word of God works quickly. It is sharp and powerful. It enables us to understand our manner of thinking. Understanding the Word of God doesn't make us mind readers, it just teaches us about human nature and helps us to understand what is in our hearts.

Sleepless nights and guilt ridden days are not evidence of success. We may possess power, position and wealth but if our hearts are not right, we are unable to enjoy our accomplishments. No amount of worldly success can satisfy a restless spirit.

With God in control of my life I can avail myself of all His resources. This enables me to be all that He wants me to be for all the days He gives me upon the earth.

Reading my Bible one day, I came across the book of Isaiah. I thought this was a complicated book. Hard to understand. I noticed in the 53rd chapter and the 6th verse "All we like sheep have gone astray; we have turned every one to his own way; and the LORD hath laid on him the iniquity of us all." All we like sheep . . . Why did God compare man to sheep? He had all the animals of the world available to him and yet he chose sheep. There must be a reason for this comparison. I knew nothing about sheep and had never known one person interested in studying them.

Since God declares man to be like sheep, I decided to study sheep to get to know me! This book contains the information I learned about sheep and shepherds and how we as people compare to sheep and relate to a shepherd (GOD).

Sheep Need Full-Time Supervision

Sheep are the only herd animals that require full-time supervision. When a man decides to raise them he must commit his life to them. Other herd animals can be fenced, fed, watered and checked on occasionally and they will probably be fine. Not so with sheep! They must be watched during the day and secured at night. In the Middle Eastern countries, the shepherds bring their sheep into the house at night.

I sat on a wall in the old city of Jerusalem and watched the shepherds lead their sheep into the fields. They walked them out of the city in the early morning and in the late afternoon you would find them walking back into the city.

I rode a bus through the hillside to the Dead Sea and saw the nomadic Bedouins in the fields watching their flock. They spent the entire day walking among the sheep. What a tiring, thankless job that seemed to be.

Since God compares men with sheep, as sheep, men need full-time supervision. Men are not like cows who can be put out to pasture. They are not like fish who swim around unnoticed. Men need to be cared for and supervised.

In the Old Testament days before Jesus was born, God had chosen certain men to be leaders of men. When the children of Israel were in bondage to the people of Egypt, God selected Moses to lead these people to freedom.

Moses was in the field caring for the sheep of his father-in-law when God called him to go and tell the Egyptian pharaoh to let His people go.

Moses was going to have a hard job leading 2 million murmuring people through a desert for 40 years. God never sends His man unprepared. Moses received training as he cared for the sheep. He learned to care patiently and constantly for the sheep. When God gave him orders, Moses switched from sheep to men. Since we are all like sheep, Moses had learned a great deal about human nature while caring for sheep.

David was a young boy when God picked him to be the King of Israel. He was picked to be the king, but he was sent back into the fields to keep the flock.

David knew from experience that sheep need full-time supervision, and he must have learned that man did too! He wrote in the all-time favorite 23rd Psalm: The Lord is my shepherd, I shall not want...

In John 10:11 Jesus said, "I am the good shepherd; the good shepherd giveth his life for the sheep." Jesus became our shepherd. He was willing to give constant supervision to His people who were like sheep. Jesus refers to himself as the door of the sheep fold. He said, "I am the door: by me if any man enter in, he shall be saved, and shall go in and out and find pasture." John 10:9

Have you ever wondered why Jesus called Himself the door? A man once observed a Bedouin shepherd at the close of a day, leading his sheep into a rock enclosure. He was impressed with the shepherd's concern for the safety of the sheep. He noticed there was no door for the enclosure.

When asked about the door, the shepherd replied, "I sleep in the doorway. I myself am the door. None of the sheep come out except with my permission and no wolves can enter in unless they pass me first. I am the door." What security this should give to us! Jesus is the door. Nothing can get to us without passing through Him!

Sheep Need Full-Time Supervision Because They Are Not Trainable!

Characteristics of Sheep

Sheep need full-time supervision because they are not trainable. Their problem is they never learn from mistakes. They do the same dumb things over and over, again and again. Trainable animals are those that learn from mistakes. They respond to punishment and they remember pain. Sheep don't remember anything. You never see sheep performing on television or in a circus. They go astray and get in trouble. Despite this, they continue to stray from the shepherd's care.

A Shepherd's Care

Knowledgeable shepherds are aware that sheep are not trainable. A shepherd must commit himself to the constant care of his flock. He must honor this commitment day and night for the life of the sheep since he knows that the sheep don't remember. Pain and punishment have no effect on future behavior.

THIS IS ONE REASON FOR A SHEPHERD'S COMMITMENT TO FULL-TIME SUPERVISION.

Characteristics of People

When a child is labeled not trainable he is said to be custodial. For the protection and safety of the child, he must be placed in the hands of a person capable of giving special care to him.

Man has been greatly gifted by God. We have the ability to build supersonic aircraft, high rise buildings, super highways and mighty bridges. We have developed vaccines to prevent certain diseases from spreading, we have learned to count calories in food and to build computers that store billions of facts.

We can write books and plays and compose music and sing great songs, but we have trouble with our weight! We know that we should not lie but we keep on doing it in spite of all our resolutions made on New Year's Day and throughout the year. We promise ourselves and others that we will stop losing our temper and before we know what has happened, we have lost it again!

Despite all the evidence, we don't like thinking of ourselves as being custodial. That is a bad sounding word. With all our God given gifts and talents, we find it hard to believe that we need to put ourselves in the total care of anyone, God included!

Several years ago I went on a diet. I was successful. I lost 25 pounds and I really looked good. My friends would stop me on the street and ask me how I lost all my weight. I would laugh and say, "I stopped eating." Now that is not exactly true, but I did stop eating too much food. I cut back on my calorie intake and burned more calories than I ate. The ounces began to fall off. Slowly but surely my clothes began to fit better. After 7 months of being hungry, I had lost my 25 pounds.

Now that I was at my desired weight I could forget about dieting and enjoy food. Several months later I popped a button off my new skirt. I quickly sewed it on again. Several days later I slid into the center section of the back seat of my car and that same button popped off for the second time.

I was really annoyed with myself for not being able to sew a simple button on a skirt. I found some quilting thread in my sewing box and decided to use it. Now that button would stay put! To my amazement the knot on the quilting thread pulled through the fabric of my skirt.

I had to face the truth. The trouble with the button was not my sewing. I now had to get the courage to look in the full-length mirror behind my bedroom door. It was even harder to get the courage to step on the bathroom scales. The sad fact was made evident. Ten pounds had returned!

I was so mad at my metabolism that I decided to forget it and move the buttom to the end of the skirt belt. Forget scales and starving. My metabolism was such that I was just going to be over-weight!

I soon got tired of a thick waist line and went back to being hungry. I lost 10 pounds. I have repeated this cycle more than twice in my fifty years of life. I just don't seem to learn from my mistakes. I find myself doing the same dumb things over and over and over, again and again and again.

For many years, the latest diet book has been found listed in the top ten best selling books in America. Could it be there are others with my same problem? I need full-time supervision to remind me what to eat and how much. I need a special kind of discipline to do what I know I should do!

The truth will set you free!

I have another problem. This one is lying. I am getting better but several months ago my husband and I agreed not to repeat something we had heard. I went right out and repeated it. That night as we were standing before our separate closets hanging up our clothes and getting ready for bed, Sam asked me if I repeated it! I was amazed at how quickly I said, "No"! Sam believed me!

I finished hanging up my clothes and went into the bathroom to brush my teeth. Closing the door I turned and there was my face in the mirror, looking back at me. I suddenly felt hot all over. I realized that Sam would find out what I had done. He would know. It might be tomorrow or next week or next month but he would find out. It might even take six months but he would find out. I was going to dread seeing my husband and even dread his phone calls.

I could picture it. Sam would come home late and tired. He would slowly walk up the sidewalk to our front door, carrying his briefcase. His head would be bowed. I would hear him and look out the front window to be sure it was Sam. When I saw his downtrodden appearance I would know that now he had found out what I did!

If it did not happen that way, he would call me on the telephone and his voice would sound low and tired. The minute I would hear him I would be sure that NOW he has found out.

I buried my head in my hands. I was trapped. I hate having to hide something from Sam. I could not face the next days or weeks or even months because of my lie. I must say that I was not sorry I broke our agreement. I was sorry I was now about to get caught in a lie!

What I had done could not be undone. I had told somebody something we agreed we would not tell. You cannot take back words. Does God offer help for a situation such as mine? Is there a way to correct part of my mistake? How can God help me now?

The Shepherd's Care

My maintenance manual, the Bible, teaches me what to do about telling lies. First, I learned that God calls it "sin". That seems to be a harsh word! I John 1:9 explains what to do about sin. "If we confess our sin, God is faithful and just to forgive us our sins and to cleanse us from all unrighteousness." Confess means to admit oneself guilty of what one is accused of. It is a result of inward conviction. I wanted to justify my lie and say I did it so Sam would not lecture me. I wanted to stay out of trouble and lying is one of the easiest ways to accomplish that goal. I had to be willing to admit my guilt and agree with God. He would do the rest! He would forgive and cleanse my heart. I bowed my head and agreed that I had been wrong and I thanked Him for His faithfulness to take this sin from me.

Now I had to clear up this matter with Sam. He was in bed almost asleep. I climbed in the bed and snuggled close to him. I put my head on his shoulder and reached my right arm around his chest and pulled him close to me. He was enjoying this. I said, "Sam, I have something to tell you." Tenderly, He said, "What?" I said, "I lied to you!" He sat up in bed, looked at me with a strange look and asked, "why"! I told him I lied because I did not want a lecture from him! He laughed, laid down and went to sleep. We never mentioned the incident again except when I use it as an illustration in my seminars or in my counseling. I hate lying. I wish I could promise I will not tell another lie. It was so easy for me to do. I lied so quickly. I need that inward convicting work of the Holy Spirit to make me aware of my sin. This comes as a result of having Jesus Christ in control of my life, having Him as my Shepherd leading me. I need to hear that still small voice somewhere inside of me calling my attention to my mistakes. Without this guidance, I keep doing the same dumb things over and over and over, again and again and again.

I can write a book and cook a great meal. I can drive a car and keep my house clean. I find it difficult to control my tongue. I say things I know I should not say. I eat things I should not be eating. I have been doing this for years. I need help! Jesus Christ, the Good Shepherd, wants to give me that guidance and help! He is patient and will work patience in me. He will be my strength. I resist supervision but I need it. Like sheep, I go astray and want to have my own way. I need a shepherd to watch over me and keep me in his care. Many times I do not want anyone leading me. I am afraid I won't be able to get what I want. I turn from The Shepherd and go my own independent way, thinking if I ignore Him, He will not see what I am doing.

Deceitful Duffie

When we lived in the Philippines, we had a Doberman dog to guard our house. Duffie was very large, very strong and very smart. She learned how to open our front screen door. She would strike it sharply with her paw and it would open just enough for her to get her nose between the door and the door frame. With a quick whip of her head, she could enter our living room.

We raised bananas in our yard. Our house girl cut the stalk when the bananas were green and hung them upside down to ripen. Duffie loved bananas. They hung in the kitchen. Duffie knew she was not allowed to come into the house to get her food. She was fed in the back yard.

One day while we were sitting in the living room, Duffie popped open the screen door, ran through the house into the kitchen. We sat quietly and waited to see what she was up to!

In a few minutes, Duffie walked through the room with her head turned away from us. She had a large ripe banana in her mouth.

We roared with laughter as we realized what she was doing. Duffie was smart enough to open the door and go for a banana and dumb enough to believe if she did not look at us, we would not see her banana.

As strong, smart human beings, we often believe if we ignore God, He won't see us with "our bananas"!

It's hard to train a dog and it's even harder to train a person. Since we don't learn from our mistakes, training is difficult. It should be obvious, being like sheep, we need full time supervision!

Sheep Need Full-Time Supervision Because They Are Afraid To Drink From Running Water!

Characteristics of Sheep

Sheep are afraid to drink from running water. Still water is sometimes stagnant and harmful. Sheep are not even aware of their need for water. They are often found grazing beside the water with early signs of dehydration.

A Shepherd's Care

An experienced shepherd is aware that sheep must be led to safe water. He must watch each animal to make sure it drinks. Often he resorts to the use of his crook to aid them to begin to drink.

Sheep aren't conscious of their dependence on the shepherd. They nibble away at blades of green grass, staying away from the running water. They can be suffering from a lack of water and be afraid to drink.

ANOTHER REASON FOR THE SHEPHERD TO HONOR HIS COMMITMENT AND PROVIDE FULL-TIME SUPERVISION FOR THE SHEEP.

Characteristics of People

As a teenager I could hardly wait to graduate from high school and leave my loving, caring thoughtful parents. I felt restless and thought going away to college would calm that restless spirit. I wanted to be on my own. I was thirsty for freedom.

Arriving at the university, I found I had to do my own laundry, find my own food, manage my money and on top of all this responsibility, I had to study! I soon got tired of the dormitory life and the "rah rah" gang. That restlessness had followed me to college. My thirst had not been satisfied.

I needed to graduate and get a job and be on my own with nobody telling me what to do. I graduated and got a job. I made $158.20 each month and paid $60.00 apartment rent.

I found myself in a financial bind. I had too much pride to let my parents know of my struggles. I had to have at least two dinner dates each week to survive. This life style did not turn out to be satisfying! I was still thirsty!

In November of my first year of teaching school, I met a third year dental student. He was a special guy and I fell in love with him on the second date. He fell in love with me on the first date! We spent every spare minute together and when he asked me to marry him, he promised me everything but the moon! He told me I was wonderful and the greatest girl he had ever dated. He promised to spend the rest of his life making me happy. I believed him! We became engaged 7 weeks after we met and we married 6 months after our engagement.

After a glorious honeymoon we went to our new apartment and settled in for Sam to finish his last year of dental school. I continued to teach fourth grade in the public school. I had failed to realize that after we married, Sam was not going home. I had to wash his clothes, iron his shirts, plan his meals, purchase and cook his food. I had to drive him to school, pick him up each afternoon and account to him for every penny I spent.

I cried each afternoon as I ironed those terrible dental jackets with all those front and back pleats. I was smart and I would figure out a way to get out of all this work. I would get pregnant. Surely Sam would get me a maid and I would not have to do all this terrible house work. I did not feel very satisfied in this new relationship. I was still thirsty!

I got pregnant but I still had to do all the work. Now I cried and threw up as I ironed. To make a long story short, in my search for satisfaction I ended up with three babies in thirty-four months and no help with the housework, the cooking or caring for the children.

All of my fulfilled goals failed to satisfy the thirsting inside of me. I began to wish I had never been born. I was miseragble and as I looked at my life, there was no apparent reason for my misery.

I felt desperate. Sam and I had no time alone. (We were bored with each other anyway.) He worked hard at the office and did not like bringing problems home. He did not want to hear about my problems in raising his children so we had very little to say to each other.

On occasion we would go out to dinner and end up sitting alone, face to face staring at the napkin or the plate. I hated my life.

Miserable among the happy

I was invited to a Bible class and definitely did not want to go. I was not interested in religion and did not like people who were. For two years my faithful friend kept inviting me. Finally, I accepted just to shut her up. This was a couples class so I arranged for a baby sitter. I made plans to meet friends after the class so Sam would not be too mad at me for dragging him to this class.

When Sam came in from the office I announced our plans. (With my back to him.) I did not want to see his face when I told him we were going to a Bible class. He did not say one word.

We went to the class. I felt uncomfortable being there. There were fifty happy people in one room. It is not much fun to be miserable and walk into a room of happy people. One man in the rear of the room kept saying "amen" as loud as could be. I felt that I was out of place. These were not my kind of people.

We left that group and met our friends and I had 6 drinks to forget that terrible experience. We got in our car and drove to the country club and never mentioned the class. Sam and I had never prayed together and never read the Bible because religion had no place in our relationship. It was personal, private and very embarrassing to mention God, especially the name of Jesus.

The next morning found me in bed with a hangover. Sam had gone to the office and the children were watching television and scattering cereal over the den floor. I lay in the bed wishing I could go back to sleep when suddenly out of nowhere a Bible verse flashed across the screen of my mind. Jesus said, "I am come that they might have life, and that they might have it more abundantly." John 10:10b

The Shepherd's Care

What did it mean that Jesus would give me an abundant life? How could He? I got out of the bed to look for my old college Bible. I had a few questions that needed to be answered. How could a man who died almost 2,000 years ago help me? I realized in a flash that an abundant life was all I ever wanted. I tried college and friends and a job and a husband and children. None of these things seemed to provide consistent satisfaction. Now I am faced with the fact: Jesus Christ (I knew He was God and that He would not lie) had promised me what I wanted.

I locked the bedroom door and closed the curtains. If my children saw me reading the Bible and if they told their dad, he might think I was crazy.

I grew up believing that if you were too serious about religion you would go crazy. People who believed and studied the Bible were

narrow and thought they were the only ones who knew the truth. I prided myself on being broad-minded and I wanted to continue in that manner of thinking. I wanted to hear what everyone had to say and consider their opinions as I formed my own.

I did not know anything about this Book but I was aware that one of the books was named John. Turning there I read the 4th chapter. I found myself intrigued with what I was reading.

This was the story of Jesus and a woman of Samaria. The woman had come to draw water and Jesus was sitting beside the well. He asked her for a drink. She seemed to know from His appearance that he was Jewish. The Jewish people did not speak to the Samaritans. This woman was shocked that Jesus spoke to her.

Jesus said if she knew who He was, she would ask Him for water. He explained that the water from this earthly well would temporarily satisfy her thirst. She would soon have to drink again. Then He said, "whosoever drinketh of this water shall thirst again: but whosoever drinketh of the water that I shall give him shall never thirst; but the water that I shall give him shall be in him a well of water springing up into everlasting life." John 4:13 & 14

The woman said to Him, "Sir, give me this water, that I thirst not, neither come hither to draw." John 4:15

I sat back in my chair. I remember saying, "God, I am so tired of trying to find satisfaction in life. I am so sick of struggling to satisfy my thirst. I am so ashamed that I have so much and it is not enough. God, if Jesus can give this woman a drink that will satisfy her forever, could He give me one, too? I don't understand all this but I want an abundant life and I want my life to count for something so if you could do this for me, I want you to."

That is all I said, no amen, no kneeling. I just sat in my chair with my head back and my eyes open.

Changed by the Shepherd

I was not aware that anything happened to me that day. Several days later I was cleaning my house and I realized I was enjoying it. Later I was washing dishes with a song in my heart. I must be sick. How could a college graduate enjoy such mundane chores as washing dishes and dusting furniture!

My children did not get on my nerves as they had before. I actually had a song in my heart for no reason. Nothing had changed about my life style but something was different inside of me.

The grass looked greener and the sky seemed more beautiful. The flowers were more apparent to me. I had never noticed their brilliant colors.

I began to have an interest in reading the Bible. I was so shocked at my interest and my understanding of it. I did not want anyone to know that I was sitting home reading the Bible. I lied to my friends when they called to ask what I was doing.

As I read this book, I began to realize that Christianity is not a way of life. It is a man. It is the person of Jesus Christ. He will satisfy the thirsty feelings deep inside of man.

One day I read a quote from a French physicist, Pascal, "In the heart of every man is a God-shaped vacuum that cannot be filled by anything created but by God the Creator made known through Jesus Christ."

I got so excited. This quote answered many of my questions. Why did I feel so good? What was happening to me? I understood that I had been trying to fill that vacuum with people, things, events, places and nothing fit. I felt that I had a round hole inside of me and I had been taking square pegs and trying to force them to fit that round hole.

Jesus Christ the Good Shepherd, wants to satisfy me. He leads me beside the still waters and He restoreth my soul.

My soul is that part of me that communicates with my fellow man. I can be satisfied with my relationships. God will change my heart and give me the qualities of life that will cause me to be satisfied with myself. I can be loving, joyful, peaceful, contented and patient. These are the characteristics of Jesus Christ and He now offers to cause me to be like Him.

The woman at the well said to Jesus, "Give me this water to drink so that I will not thirst again and I will not have to come and draw water from this well." It is a burdensome task in the heat of the day to carry a heavy water pot back into the city.

Jesus revealed who He was to this woman. He met her at her point of need. She got so excited she left her water pot and ran into the city to tell the people about Jesus.

Her excitement rested in the fact that she had found a consistent source to satisfy her thirst. Many places in the Bible show water as a symbol of the Word of God.

While grazing by the creek, sheep get preoccupied with the food they want and are blind to their need for the water nearby.

In attempting to satisfy our wants we often find ourselves spiritually dehydrated. When we turn to the Bible we find the water that we need.

We, like sheep, need a shepherd who will lead us to the satisfying still water.

Sheep Need Full-Time Supervision Because They Are Led, Not Driven!

Characteristics of Sheep

Sheep have a natural tendency to follow a leader. Attempts to drive them causes sheep to scatter. They move from one location to another in a group. Sheep recognize the voice of their shepherd and respond to his call. They depend more on their ears than their eyes for recognizing their shepherd. It is important that they spend time with the shepherd to become familiar with his voice. Familiarity builds confidence in the shepherd.

A Shepherd's Care

Any shepherd attempting to drive his flock soon becomes frustrated because the sheep begin to scatter. An experienced shepherd understands the tendency of sheep and always walks before them. The shepherd talks to the sheep on a regular basis to enable them to be familiar with his voice. It is important for him to be near the sheep to enable them to hear when he speaks. Because the shepherd leads them where their needs are met and protects them at all times, he builds strong confidence in the sheep.

ANOTHER REASON FOR THE SHEPHERD TO HONOR HIS COMMITMENT AND PROVIDE FULL-TIME SUPERVISION FOR THE SHEEP!

Characteristics of People

Sheep can't be driven and neither can man. Most parents have to learn the hard way that they can't force their children to go where they would have them go. They can lead them there but it takes time and patience.

Children, like sheep, are going to follow someone and they usually follow in groups. I watched my son get in a group and become a leader. I discouraged the relationship because of the activities of the group. I begged and punished and cried but I could not make him change his friendships.

After all we had done for him and now he was getting involved with the wrong crowd. One morning Mark refused to get out of bed to go to work. Sam went into his room and screamed at him. This was really out of character for Sam because he is not a screamer. I could see the resentment Sam had toward Mark.

Mark jumped out of the bed, threw on his clothes and ran out the front door. I did what all good mothers do, sat down and cried. Sam was in the bathroom shaving. I knew that Mark was going to run away. This was the one thing I was afraid I could not emotionally handle.

Sam came out of the bathroom and saw me crying. This is the one thing Sam can't stand up to emotionally. "Just be happy" is his motto.

He did not want me to cry. It was a bad scene. Sam was "fed up" with Mark's laziness. Now Sam was mad at me for crying and at Mark for sleeping late.

I love Sam and appreciate his good qualities. I looked at him and realized that I wanted Mark to follow his dad. I did not know of another man I would recommend Mark follow. I want Mark to follow the Lord and I felt he needed a role model!

In those few tense minutes, I began to think about the people that influence my life. I knew without having to give it much thought that they are the people who love me. They are the people who love me unconditionally and accept me just as I am!

Sam and I discussed how we must accept Mark just as he is, with all his bad habits and attitudes. We need to be an example before him and lead by loving him. Mark had wandered from the fold and needed to be led back. As parents, we needed to follow our Shepherd and let Him lead us as we lead our son.

Sam and I prayed and asked God to forgive us for the resentment we felt for our son. We asked God to fill our hearts with love and acceptance for Mark. Sam telephoned Mark at work. He said he was sorry for the way he had talked to him.

Mark quickly accepted his dad's apology and apologized for his behavior. Mark knew he was wrong. He knew his dad should get him out of bed and send him to work. Mark also knew his dad was wrong in the way he did it.

That was the day Sam began to lead Mark. It took five years for us to see a change in Mark. We had told him that we did not approve of his life style. We did not need to keep telling him over and over and over and over. He is a smart guy and he heard and understood the first time we said it.

We never backed down on our stand or compromised our standards but we loved Mark and let him know we were here when he needed us. We wanted Mark's home to be a place of peace where he could come and find acceptance. He need never be afraid or ashamed to come home.

A splitting headache

One of my greatest experiences as a mother came in a most unusual way. The night before Mark graduated from high school, he got in a fight. The only one I knew about. He went to a graduation party that we gave him permission to go to. One of the guys hosting the party got drunk and started to fight one of Mark's friends. Mark is 6 feet tall. His friend was 5 feet 9 inches and the host was 6 feet 2 inches. Mark stepped in to help his friend and the host's friend came down on the top of Mark's head with a bottle.

Mark's head split open. Mark tried to defend himself when three boys threw him to the ground and started kicking him. Mark managed to break away from the guys and ran through the woods for more than a mile. Blood covered his head and his body. He ran to a house and the lady inside allowed him to use her telephone. Mark called home!

The telephone rang at 11:30 p.m. Mark said, "Mom, I have been hurt, will you come get me?" I told Sam what Mark had said. Sam jumped out of bed, threw on his clothes and went for him.

We had to take him to the hospital emergency room to have stitches in his head. When the word got out among his group, one of his friends said, "I can't believe you called your mom. She would have been the last person in the world I would have called."

The Shepherd's Care

I thank God that Mark wanted to call home. No one loves our children as Sam and I. Nobody is going to take the time or go to the expense to do for them as we do. Mark was returning to the fold.

God is looking for leaders today who will feed His sheep. Leaders who will lead the sheep to Him so that He can provide for them. John 13:35 "By this shall all men know that ye are my disciples, if ye have love one to another."

It is much more exciting to go outside our homes to be a leader. We get little if any praise or appreciation for the labor of love done with the small flock gathered around the dinner table.

Sam and I decided that we wanted our children to know that God is love and that He desires that our love increase and abound for each other. God causes this to happen. The best way to teach them is by example. They need to see us turn to God for love and see us expect Him to cause our love for them to increase. To know that our love is not dependent on their behavior or their appreciation of us.

We want our children to believe that God is faithful to provide our needs when we follow Him.

When we follow Jesus Christ, our Shepherd, we can recommend our life style to others. Paul writes in Philippians 4:9, "Those things, which ye have both learned, and received, and heard, and see in me, do: and the God of peace shall be with you."

Paul was actually suggesting that people listen to his words and watch what he did and do the same. Can you say that? Sheep are led, not driven. God doesn't drive us. He leads us. The 23rd Psalm, 3rd verse says, "He restoreth my soul: he leadeth me in the paths of righteousness for his name's sake."

Some people think they are fine without a shepherd. Undisturbed, these people do well. When disturbance occurs and they must deal with upheaval in their lives, fear often sets in. With no leadership man becomes frustrated and unsure of himself.

During those quiet undisturbing days of our lives, we have a tendency to believe things will stay that way. Life is full of surprises! Some good and some bad. With the shepherd at the helm there is no fear or confusion.

When we follow the leadership of the Lord, He is pleased with our leadership of men. His name is glorified. This is not to say that when we follow the Lord, we never do anything wrong again. It is to say, He teaches us how to correct our mistakes. As others watch us, they learn how to correct their mistakes. God never expects us to be perfect but He does ask that we perfectly obey his commands. We follow Him and let Him forgive us when we sin, lead us to the water of His Word where our souls are satisfied, and He will make us leaders of men.

Sheep Need Full-Time Supervision Because When They Are On Their Backs They Cannot Right Themselves!

Characteristics of Sheep

When sheep fall and roll over onto their spine, they do not have the ability to get up. All their kicking and bleating doesn't help. While on their back they can't follow the shepherd, even though they hear his voice. They become isolated from the flock and they are easy prey for their enemies. They suffer from being in this position. Sheep can't help each other back on their feet. Only the shepherd can help. (Notice the wise sheep suggesting he get the shepherd!)

A Shepherd's Care

The shepherd must keep an eye on the sheep to make sure they stay on their feet. A knowledgeable shepherd is aware of the need to keep the sheep in the fold and of their absolute dependence on him to stay on their feet. He must be in hearing range to hear their cries and respond. In order for the shepherd to effectively lead, the sheep must be in position to follow.

ANOTHER REASON FOR THE SHEPHERD TO HONOR HIS COMMITMENT AND PROVIDE FULL-TIME SUPERVISION FOR THE SHEEP!

Characteristics of People

Many people fall down and can't get up. In 1976 the American Medical Society declared that 82% of the people in hospitals were suffering from psychosomatic illnesses.

These people were really sick. There was no physical reason for the basic cause of their illness. They are down and can't get up.

Emotional disturbances can cause bodily harm. We can become ill because of the problems of the day. We won't be faking it. We will be sick. When the doctor finds no reason for the basic cause of the illness, counseling is recommended.

Life is filled with unexpected events. I have decided it is full of disappointments. We think we are organized and things fall apart. We look forward to middle age when the children are grown and gone and we can settle back and enjoy the evening newspaper.

Middle age finds us looking after our elderly parents and we find that our children don't grow up and leave home. They multiply and come back! Sam and I have three generations of people looking to us for assistance and counsel!

Life is going to cause us to encounter severe blows. There will be times when these blows can knock us down. The issue is not being knocked down but how long before we recover. The shepherd keeps going and the sheep can't follow while on its back. We need to understand why we fall and how to get up. We fall in response to the blows of life: the sudden death of a loved one, an unexpected financial reversal, divorce, disappointment in a child's behavior, an affair, etc.

When tragedy strikes and disappointments come our way we need to know how to turn to the shepherd so that he can get us on our feet and back into the mainstream of life as quickly as possible.

We need to learn how to get help before we need it. Usually in the midst of trouble, we panic and our thinking is not clear.

An unexpected shock

In August of 1986, Dr. Henry Brandt and his wife Marcy came to visit us. Dr. Brandt is a Christian counselor, author and popular conference speaker. He has been our friend for more than 20 years but I had not met Marcy. Henry and Marcy had been married 4 years. She and I had a wonderful time together. I loved Marcy. We developed a great friendship from the start.

Henry was speaking at a Men's retreat and Marcy and I went shopping. Henry would be home that night. I wanted my friend Jane to meet her so we went by Jane's house.

We had tea and cookies and I asked Marcy to tell Jane and her husband, Jim how she met Henry. As Marcy was telling her story, she suddenly grabbed her head with both hands. She looked at me and said, "Something has happened to me!" It was obvious that she was in a great deal of pain. She asked Sam to help her. We laid her on the floor and called the paramedics. As these men worked with Marcy we watched as she slowly became unconscious and her vital signs became irratic. Sam told me that we were losing her. We prayed for God to give us wisdom and guide the doctors as they treated her.

Sam rode in the ambulance to the hospital. Jane and I went to find Henry. My heart was beating so fast I thought I would faint. I trembled as I walked into the hotel to tell him what had happened.

I remember seeing him come through the door into the lobby and suddenly my heart slowed down. I was calm as could be. Henry had been my teacher. He taught me to trust the Lord in the good times so when the bad times come, I will keep on trusting Him.

I told him Marcy was seriously ill and Sam had taken her to the hospital. Henry got in the back seat of Jane's car. Jane was driving and I was sitting beside her. We were silent. Henry's voice suddenly broke the silence, "Lord, you have promised in your word that you would comfort us in our tribulation and give us peace in times of trouble. We have trouble and tribulation so Lord we are asking you to comfort us and give us your peace. Amen."

No one spoke. We arrived at the hospital and the doctor told Henry that Marcy was gone. She had suffered a massive cerebral hemorrhage. The doctor explained that Marcy had a weak area in one of the blood vessels in her head. She could have had this all her life. It could not be detected and there is nothing that could have been done to correct the weakness. Henry cried and then turned to us and said, "I don't know what I am going to do without Marcy. I committed my life to the Lord 40 years ago. He has been faithful to me and I know He will not fail me now. Marcy has been a faithful companion to me. I will miss her." Henry had been in the habit of allowing God to pick him up when the events of life knocked him down. Henry Brandt went on doing what he had become accustomed to doing.

I am glad that I had the privilege of being with Henry those few hard days. I watched a man who had been leading me, follow his own advice.

None of us knows what the day will bring. We need to practice turning to God in the small disappointments of life so when big disappointments come our way, we will keep on doing what we are in the habit of doing.

I had a friend who had cancer. She was not a Christian and many people had prayed for her for years. Many said, "Now she will turn to the Lord. God is going to answer our prayers."

I watched as this lady did what she was in the habit of doing. She was very wealthy and could purchase anything she wanted or go any place she chose.

When the doctor told her that she had cancer her reply was, "No problem, I have plenty of money and I can go anywhere in the world for treatment. I will spend every penny I have to find a cure!"

My friend died trying to find a cure for this dreaded disease. I never once heard that she turned to the Lord. When she was flat on her back, she had no shepherd to call upon. Not only did she not have a shepherd, she never seemed interested in finding Him!

I know many people who have had an untimely death in their family and they have never recovered from the shock nor have they gotten over the grief and bitterness.

What a sad thing that we spend our time preparing financially for the future and caring for our body by going to exercise classes three times each week. We take our vitamins and count calories and forget about our spiritual life.

We don't think being spiritually prepared for the events of the day is important. When a blow comes and we find ourselves on our back, if we have not been following the Shepherd, it is unlikely that we will turn to him for help. Often our guilt makes us feel ashamed to ask for help.

The Shepherd's Care

In II Corinthians chapter 4 verse 7 The Living Bible says: "But this precious treasure—this light and power that now shines within us—is held in a perishable container, that is, in our weak bodies. Everyone can see that the glorious power within must be from God and is not our own." In verses 9 and 10: "We are hunted down, but God never abandons us. We get knocked down, but we get up again and keep going. These bodies of ours are constantly facing death just as Jesus did; so it is clear to all that it is only the living Christ within (who keeps us safe)."

We need a strong confidence in the shepherd while we are on our feet. Should we find ourselves on our backs, that strong confidence will motivate us to call to Him to put us back on our feet and keep us moving as He leads us throughout life.

When on our backs, we, like sheep, need a Shepherd!

Sheep Need Full-Time Supervision Because They Are Not Burden Bearing Animals!

Characteristics of Sheep

Sheep are not physically able to carry heavy loads. You will never see one hitched to a wagon or carrying a load on its back. A heavy load would break the back of a sheep. They seem to follow behind the shepherd without a care. They don't even know where they are going.

A Shepherd's Care

The shepherd bears the burden of finding pasture and fresh water for the sheep. He leads them to safety day and night. A caring shepherd has made preparation for the day. He knows where to find pasture and water before he starts leading his sheep. When the sheep have no concern for their needs they seem to follow the shepherd more closely and stay in the flock.

ANOTHER REASON FOR THE SHEPHERD TO HONOR HIS COMMITMENT AND PROVIDE FULL-TIME SUPERVISION FOR THE SHEEP!

Characteristics of People

God compares men with sheep. This being so, men were not designed to bear burdens. In the Living Bible I Peter chapter 5 verse7: "Let Him have all your worries and cares, for He is always thinking about you and watching everything that concerns you." Notice the three words used in this verse that could only be stated by an all powerful omniscient God:

1) He doesn't want some of your worries, but **all** of them,

2) He is not sometimes thinking about you but **always,**

3) He is not watching some of the things that concern you, but **everything.**

Does this excite you? It should!

Worry causes fatigue. To worry is to become disturbed, tense and troubled. The use of the word "cares" in I Peter means to be anxious and to endure emotional pain from the apprehension of evil.

When we worry our muscles become tense. We jump at the simple sound of a telephone ringing. Our body does not function properly. Headaches, stomach aches and a spastic colon are common. Things go from bad to worse. It is hard to concentrate when you are in pain or bodily discomfort.

God has offered to take our cares and worries. He made us, knows all about us and desires the best for us. Psalms 34:10

Emotional strain-physical change

My daughter, Dawn had a convulsion when she was ten months old. I had never seen a person in this condition and I thought she had died in my arms. Her beautiful brown eyes were fixed in a stare, her little mouth was open and her precious body was rigid. When I saw my baby in this condition I became hysterical. I was not able to help care for her. God was gracious and had Sam home with me when this happened. I started screaming. Sam took the baby to the kitchen and began to work with her. He was screaming for me to help him and I was just standing in the living room with my head in my hands, screaming as loud as I could. Some neighbors heard me and ran to help.

I was paralyzed with fear. My child needed me and I could not function. My neighbor called the doctor and my husband cared for the baby. I was useless. For years I lived with the memory of this day. I was ashamed of my behavior and surprised at my weakness. I wondered what mental condition I would have been in had she died. I was tormented by these memories.

Months later I ended up in the doctor's office with a spastic colon. My doctor explained to me that the pain was caused by tension so he gave me tranquilizers to relieve my pain. I was glad for that little pill. When I felt the pain begin in my abdomen, I took the pill. It worked. The pain would always subside. I never knew when I would experience an attack so I never left home without the pills.

When I became a Christian I realized that God loved me enough to die for me. I also realized that He loved my children in the same way. He even loves them more than I do. That seemed impossible but I knew it was true. This being the case, I found it easy to trust Him with their lives. I have been given the privilege of caring for them while they are young but He bears the responsibility for them. Although I can't always go with them, He does, although I can't see them 24 hours each day, He does.

My children are Christians, God is their heavenly Father. He is their Shepherd. Should they die before me, I know they will go to be with Him and one day we will be together. Words are not adequate to express the freedom I felt when this began to make sense to me. I truly felt that a heavy weight had been taken from my shoulders. I seemed to be able to breathe easier!

I pray daily for the safety of my family. I ask God to keep them from harm. I want them to live long healthy lives but now I know if God takes them before He takes me, I can trust Him. I no longer live with the torment of fear.

Now I was free to enjoy my children. I no longer felt panic over what would happen to them. The pain in my abdomen went away.

If you have ever had a spastic colon, you know it completely debilitates you. I know now that my suffering was totally unnecessary except for what it taught me. I learned that worry and the tension resulting from it can cause pain and bodily harm.

To cast your cares on the Lord does not mean you are not interested. It doesn't mean you are not involved in finding solutions to problems. It simply means you are not anxious during your involvement. You have the choice of being anxiously involved or peacefully involved.

A down in the mouth sheep

It is not easy to break habits. It is hard to commit burdens to the Lord when you have been bearing them for years. My husband, Sam is a dentist. He worked hard to pay his way through dental school. In order to save money, we lived on a tight budget during our three years in the U.S. Air Force. Sam would have little income as he established his private practice.

Sam opened his office and it was "slow-go" for several years. The office was closed Thursday and Saturday afternoons and all day Sunday. On two or three occasions, we took a vacation. We left at noon on Thursday and returned Sunday afternoon. This three day vacation meant that Sam was out of his office for only one and one-half working days.

We only took two or three of these three day vacations because after Friday morning, I was ready to go home. Sam was a mental wreck! He knew that one and one-half days out of the office could mean starvation for the family. I felt sorry for him. Just imagine, one wife and three small children looking to your two hands to produce enough money to house, feed, clothe and educate them. What a responsibility!

Sam was with us in body but we knew his mind was back on the appointment book. He seldom heard what we were saying, did not smile much and was short tempered with the children.

Monday was a glorious day, Sam went back to the office! I don't mean by that statement that we did not love Sam. It was just miserable having a dad around physically who was not around mentally.

Sam invited Jesus Christ to come into his life on the same day I did. We began to study the Bible and pray together. This was a new experience for us. Sam began to tell me about the burden he felt to provide for us and how he could not get rid of it. Becoming a Christian had not helped.

One afternoon on the front page of our newspaper there appeared a picture of the earth. It was the first time the earth had been photographed from outer space. The picture was in color and you could see the water masses but you could not identify the continents.

Sam walked up the driveway looking at that picture. As he came into the kitchen to show me, he realized that there was our planet suspended in space. Two-thirds of its surface was water and not one drop was spilling! God had created this universe and was in complete control of it.

Sam kept looking at the picture and realized that North America was a very small area. The United States was hard to identify. Just think how large the U.S. is and yet it could hardly be identified. Alabama could not be distinguished from the other states. Then he realized that his office was not visible. He started to laugh. "Just think," Sam said, "God can sustain the universe with every drop of water in place. My office is so small you can't see it and I have trouble believing He can handle it!"

That was the day Sam cast the burden of his practice on the Lord, knowing He cares for him. Some people say, the Lord has more important things to do than take care of a dental office. Yet the Bible teaches us that God delights in caring for His flock. He delights in leading His flock to green pastures and beside the still waters.

Sam began to commit each day to the Lord. This commitment included his appointment book as well as the collections at the end of each month. Sam's mental attitude began to change. Slowly the worry and anxiety went away. He was no less interested in his patients and his practice. He was free to enjoy his profession. The worry would return on many occasions and he would just remember that picture from outer space. Sam needed to commit each day to the Lord and trust Him to supply our needs. You can't commit a week or even tomorrow. This is something you need to do daily.

Many people turn to drugs to help relieve their burden and worry. This will give a temporary sense of peace. However, I don't recommend the use of drugs for this purpose.

Because we worry about tomorrow, we can not enjoy today! I have heard Sam say, "Don't tell me worrying doesn't help. Most of the things I worry about never happen!"

Sometimes it helps us to remember that today is the tomorrow we worried about yesterday.

The Shepherd's Care

When you cast your burden on the Lord, you trust Him to help you find answers to your problems. There is a wonderful promise in the book of James, chapter 1 verses 5-8: "If any of you lacks wisdom, let him ask of God, that giveth to all men liberally, and upbraideth not; and it shall be given him. But let him ask in faith, nothing wavering. For he that wavereth is like a wave of the sea driven with the wind and tossed. For let not that man think that he shall receive any thing of the Lord. A double minded man is unstable in all his ways."

Wisdom is knowledge experienced. Knowledge is knowing the facts. Wisdom comes from putting these facts into practice. Notice the conditions for getting wisdom: faith, no wavering, single mindedness and stability.

Ask God to give you wisdom to live each day according to His Word and to show you how to practice the things you learn from Him.

Dr. Henry Brandt once told me, "As you prayerfully commit your days to the Lord, there are no problems, only challenges." I have read the statement, "Prayer changes things". However, I believe prayer changes people and people change things! God uses us to solve difficult situations. He gives us the knowledge we need and then by the work of His Holy Spirit, He shows us how to put this knowledge into practice. It is exciting to watch Him work.

This is what it means to rest in the Lord. No mental anguish! Peace of mind and heart. This is what God has promised us in John chapter 16 verse 33: "These things I have spoken to you, that in Me you may have peace. In the world you will have tribulation; but be of good cheer, I have overcome this world".

Like sheep, we are not designed to bear burdens. As the Lord becomes our burden bearer, we are free to enjoy Him and be used by Him.

Sheep Need Full-Time Supervision Because They Must Be Sheared At The Right Time In The Right Season!

Characteristics of Sheep

The wool that protects the sheep in winter has to be removed in the summer. Too much wool prevents the body heat from dissipating. This causes the sheep to suffer and can lead to heat prostration. It is often necessary to shear them in winter. Dirt, grass and water can accumulate deep in the wool next to the skin. Should this mud-like substance freeze, it is harmful to the sheep. Sheep can't shear each other. They need to depend on the shepherd to do the shearing. When the wool is sheared, the sheep are providing for others. Wool is an absolutely unique product. Many have tried to make an imitation, but have failed.

A Shepherd's Care

The shepherd must shear the sheep. On a trip to Israel I watched a shepherd clipping his sheep. He had to have help from a small boy. The sheep was bleating and kicking like crazy. The shepherd sat on the body of the animal and the boy held the feet. It sounded like the shepherd was killing the animal. He was taking his time, knowing this procedure was necessary for the health of the sheep. The reaction of the sheep didn't hinder the performance of the shepherd. Sheep kick and bleat when sheared for the first time. They are quiet and allow the shepherd to shear them the second time. They learn from living with the shepherd that he cares for them. They trust him to do what is necessary. An experienced shepherd recognizes which sheep need shearing. He knows it is for their protection and the wool is the product or reward the shepherd has for his work.

ANOTHER REASON FOR THE SHEPHERD TO HONOR HIS COMMITMENT AND PROVIDE FULL-TIME SUPERVISION FOR THE SHEEP!

Characteristics of People

God, being our chief Shepherd, knows when and how to shear us. Most of the time we kick and scream when He takes away something we have grown comfortable with. Seldom if ever, do we understand why this happens.

Everyone gets sheared if he lives long enough. Our family got sheared when little Gil, our grandson, became ill. He was playing in my yard with his new toy when the time came to go home. I picked him up to put him in his mom's car and realized he was very warm with fever. Several days later he was diagnosed as having bacterial meningitis. The doctor looked Dawn straight in the eye and said, "Mrs. McWhorter, if your baby lives, he can be a vegetable. He can be mentally retarded, blind, deaf, paralyzed, any or all of the above. He has so much bacteria in his spinal fluid that it appears milky and I could see it with the naked eye. We have started him on an intravenous antibiotic and there is nothing more we can do. You pray for us." With this announcement, the doctor walked away. He did not mean to be unkind, he was being honest with us.

Gil was put in intensive care for 3 days and was hospitalized for 12 days. During these days Dawn and her husband, Curry were wonderful. They had great faith in God. There were many praying for this little boy. Dawn and Curry kept saying that Gil would be fine because they were trusting God.

When Gil was able to open his eyes and look around we noticed that he did not respond to sound. He could not sit up nor could he hold up his head. We propped him up in the bed to give him some juice and he fell over on his side. We all thought it was due to his weakened condition.

When Gil was physically able, he was tested. The test proved that he had lost his equilibrium and 80% of his hearing. The therapist told Dawn that this was nerve damage and it would never be any better. She said, "You can take him anywhere in the world but the nerve damage can not be repaired. You should get hearing aids and begin therapy at once. Work fast so he will not forget the few words he has learned before this illness."

Dawn was sobbing and almost hysterical. I took Gil from her arms and she grabbed her pocketbook and ran. She went home and went to bed. I did not blame her. I wanted to run with her. Looking at that precious baby in that hospital bed, I wanted to scream and kick.

Sam came immediately to the hospital. Curry went home to be with Dawn. I sat in a chair and cried. Gil was cut off from us. We could not reach him. Would he ever hear another sound? Could he ever hear us tell him we love him?

I had two pains, one for my grandchild and the other for my child. I did not want either of them to suffer. When I stopped crying I was so weak I felt I could not drive my car to Dawn's apartment. I had to sit in a chair and wait for my strength to return. I remember sitting in that chair and talking to God. I had been dealt a mighty blow and I was down. I had been sheared. My daughter and my son-in-law had been sheared. I started remembering all I had learned about sheep, how they fall down and need the shepherd to get them up on their feet. I asked God to help me. I asked Him to get me up quickly and get me on my feet so I could help my children. I needed my strength renewed.

I thought about the fact that we are all like sheep and sheep get sheared. We were comfortable with Gil being a hearing child. We did not want this part of this little boy to be taken away. Why had God allowed this to happen? This is a question that has no answer.

The Shepherd's Care

Dawn asked me this question as soon as I got to her apartment. "Mom, why has God done this to me?" I told her, "I have no idea! I know that God is love and He has our best interest at heart. This is not my desire for Gil but because I know God's love and I know He allows things to happen and can turn the bad into good, we must trust Him in this situation. Gil's hearing is gone. We wanted it back. We can scream and kick or we can be still and see God at work. The choice is ours."

I reminded Dawn of that great passage in Hebrews chapter 12. These verses had seen me through difficult times in the past. I had memorized the verses found there: "Looking unto Jesus the author and finisher of our faith; who for the joy that was set before him endured the cross, despising the shame, and is set down at the right hand of the throne of God. For consider Him that endured such contradiction of sinners against Himself, lest ye be wearied and faint in your minds. Ye have not yet resisted unto blood, striving against sin. And ye have forgotten the exhortation which speaketh unto you as unto children, My son, despise not thou the chastening of the Lord nor faint when thou art rebuked of Him; For whom the Lord loveth He chasteneth and scourgeth every son whom he receiveth. If ye endure chastening, God dealeth with you as with sons; for what son is he whom the father chasteneth not?" (verses 2-7)

In Webster's dictionary the definition of the word chasten means to inflict pain for the purpose of reclaiming an offender. I looked in Vines Expository Dictionary of New Testament Words. In the Greek language, the word chasten denotes to train children. It suggests the broad idea of education. Hebrews was written in Greek, not English. It makes a big difference in understanding the verse when you see the original meaning of this word. We did not feel God was reclaiming us as offenders but we knew we needed to be educated. The use of the word in Hebrews means educating by the infliction of calamities. This is what God is doing in our lives. Frankly, we would prefer another way of being taught but we must believe and accept the fact that God knows what He is doing and it is best for all involved.

I would go to any extreme, spend any amount of money to have Gil's hearing restored but I thank God for all the wonderful lessons He has taught me through this calamity.

Dawn and Curry were told by the doctor that Gil would soon learn to visually compensate for his loss of equilibrium. This determined little guy was soon on his feet walking. He took many a fall but he kept getting up and trying again. He now walks and runs and climbs trees like any normal three-year-old.

Before he learned to walk we had him in a playpen on the deck. His uncle Mark whistled so loud, we covered our ears. Little Gil's eyes began to glow, he smiled a big smile. He heard the whistle. We all cried because of the look of excitement on his face. This was the first sound he had heard since his illness. Gil has regained some of his hearing and with the use of hearing aids is hearing in the normal range in one ear and is considered to have a mild loss in the other. He is talking now. Each word he says brings excitement to the family. One day as he was leaving my house, I kissed him on the cheek and said, "I love you." He smiled, looked me in the eye and said, "I wove you." We cried with joy. My other two grandsons talk constantly. We find ourselves wishing they would be quiet for a few minutes! Gil has afforded us great pleasure in these last few months. We look forward to watching him grow as he overcomes this handicap.

Benefits of being in shape

God is teaching us to trust Him. One year after Gil's illness, he stuck a stick in his ear. Dawn ran to get him but was too late. He had fallen and the stick went into his ear canal and destroyed his ear drum. He had to go into the hospital and have surgery to repair the ear drum.

Curry was at work so I had to drive Dawn to the hospital. She laughed as we walked into the emergency room and said to me, "Well, mom, it is true that you never know what a day will bring."

I thought of those kicking, bleating sheep. Dawn was not running away from this scene. She was learning from it. She had spent one year in the special care of her Shepherd and she had learned that He is capable of caring for her. She trusts Him more today than she did yesterday. Her goal in life is to trust Him even more tomorrow.

God educates us as we see Him provide for us through good times as well as through bad ones. None of us wants the bad times but they will come along. In John chapter 33 verse 16 Jesus said, "These things I have spoken unto you, that in me ye might have peace. In the world ye shall have tribulation; but be of good cheer; I have overcome the world."

The same Jesus that said He is love and that He died for us, tells us the world will give us tribulation. We get pleasure from thinking about His love and we are grateful that His death affords us salvation and freedom from the penalty of sin. We consider it negative to think about having tribulation. The truth is that we must consider both sides of the coin. We need to accept the truth of what Jesus said, prepare ourselves for what might happen and trust Him to protect us in His own way. We can even cheer up as we believe He has overcome the world.

God knows what He is doing. He knows the best thing for us and He is willing to sit on us and keep clipping while we kick. He loves us so much that He will let us kick. That is real love.

God will shear us. He will take away something we have grown accustomed to having. He will do this because He knows it is best for us. It will not be something we want to give up but when we relax and accept our losses as being from the loving hand of God, we begin to learn and to grow.

For our own good, we need to trust God to take away from us what needs to be removed. We will stop fighting God as we see the benefit that comes from shearing.

The heart of this book is to help you understand the importance of being in shape because you never know when you will be sheared!

Clipping to a sheep in shape can be a shear delight!

Like sheep, we need to be sheared!

Sheep Need Full-Time Supervision Because Their Vision Is Impaired When They Are Not Sheared!

Characteristics of Sheep

Sheep can see only a short distance in front of them unless the wool is trimmed from their face. Shearing is a necessary process for the sheep. It is not a pleasant experience for them. Without it not only are they in danger of freezing or heat prostration, but their vision is limited. We can't interview sheep to determine their attitude following the shearing but we can observe the improvement in their vision. They are better able to see the provisions of the shepherd. This builds stronger confidence in their shepherd.

A Shepherd's Care

An experienced loving shepherd knows the importance of good vision. He is very interested in the sheep building confidence in him through being aware of his provisions.

ANOTHER REASON FOR THE SHEPHERD TO HONOR HIS COMMITMENT AND PROVIDE FULL-TIME SUPERVISION FOR THE SHEEP!

Characteristics of People

In 1972 Sam and I with our three children moved to Manila, Philippines to work with Campus Crusade for Christ. When Sam first told me of this opportunity, I was afraid. I wondered what it would be like to live in Asia. I was afraid to give up the financial security Sam's dental practice provided for us. I was afraid of what would happen to our children. They would not have all the material things I had planned for them. I lost sleep wrestling with these fears. I wanted to take advantage of the opportunity but I was comfortable in my life styles and afraid to give it up.

When we arrived in Manila, I could hardly believe my eyes. The airport had been burned. It was raining. It kept raining and Manila experienced the worst flood in more than 100 years. School was closed. We sat in our apartment for 3 weeks with no telephone, no television, no newspaper, no friends. We cried and begged Sam to take us home. He laughs now as he recalls that each night before we went to bed we took a vote whether to go home or stay. It was always 4 to 1! Sam's 1 vote carried and we stayed.

Finally the sun came out and school started. Living in Manila was like going back in time 100 years. The streets were full of potholes. We shopped in an open market where fly covered meat hung from the ceiling. Fish were flapping on the tables and the chickens walked around in their cages.

Often the telephone didn't work, and each day the lights unexpectedly went out for an indefinite period of time. We settled in to a nice house and soon the children began to make friends. They went to a wonderful school. The teachers were the best. There were so many activities that they found it hard to select the ones in which they wanted to get involved.

I began to see how dependent I was on "things". I couldn't go out and buy a dress for myself or a shirt for Sam. There were no ready-made clothes in our sizes. I had to purchase material, find a dressmaker and a tailor and have all our clothes made.

Nothing was easy about life in Manila. It took so much time to do anything. We lived 4 miles from the downtown area and I have spent as much as 2 hours in the car trying to get home because of the congested traffic.

Sleeping through a traffic jam

One day I sat in my new air conditioned car waiting for a traffic jam to clear up. I had been to teach a Bible class in a downtown church. My son, Sam had driven me. This was during the rainy season and the streets were flooded. Cars had to creep along or the water would cause them to stall.

It was 9:00 at night and we had not had dinner! The temperature was in the high 80's and it was raining. The humidity was so high that the air conditioning in the car had little effect on the temperature. Sam III and I sat for 15 minutes at a crowded intersection. After 5 minutes I was out of patience. I could not believe how dumb these people were. If they would only put up lights to control the traffic. If only they realized that they could not all go through this intersection at the same time.

I was so mad I was even yelling at Sam (as if he could do anything about the situation)! There was a bus waiting next to our car. You could not see through the bus because of the number of people packed in it. I saw one old lady who appeared to be in her seventies. She was packed in that bus like a sardine in a can. She could not move and I was surprised that she could even breathe. She had her hand on the bar above her head and her head was bowed. I realized she was sound asleep.

I will never forget that lady. There I was, the missionary, so mad I could hardly sit still in my new air conditioned car with the bucket seats. This dear lady was so peaceful she could sleep while standing on a hot, musty, crowded bus!

I felt convicted over my attitude. I saw myself with a new set of eyes and I was ashamed. Here I sat, impatient, selfish, mad and hostile. I will never forget that little old lady on the bus. I don't know her name, yet God used her to show me what I looked like to Him. This has happened to me many times since, and it is always terrible. Conviction is a bad feeling but a necessary one. We are blind to our sins and it takes the Spirit of God to open our eyes to see the truth about ourselves. However, I don't have much trouble seeing sin in others!

God removed the comforts of home, the pleasure of conveniences, the joy of friends and the security of family to help me see myself. It was hard going through this shearing process but now in retrospect, I "see" that it was worth it. I would not trade those few hard years for anything.

There were many days I felt our future looked bleak. I worried about how we would be able to educate our children. I worried about sending them 12,000 miles across the Pacific Ocean to college and seeing them only once every two or three years. There were times I would walk by young Sam's bedroom and cry. He was a senior in high school and I dreaded the day he would leave for college in the states. God dealt with my fearful attitude as I flew to an island south of Manila.

The Shepherd's Care

Sam and I went to the Island of Cebu to speak at a conference. We were flying on a Philippine Airlines plane. The captain's voice came over the loudspeaker. "Ladies and gentlemen, this is your captain speaking from the flight deck. Our cabin is not pressurized and we will be forced to fly at a low altitude. We will be encountering turbulence so please buckle your seat belt. We will be late arriving in Cebu. We hope you enjoy your flight!

I had my seat belt buckled so I sank down in my seat, heaved a huge sigh and talked to God. I said, "Well God, I don't care if this dumb airplane crashes. I wish I were dead anyway. I am sick of life, I don't like living in this place and I am tired of worrying about my future. I can't bear to send my children to the U.S. and be so far from them. I hate homemade clothes. I am tired of being hot. Just let this plane fall into the South China Sea and let me die and get out of this mess!

With that prayer I picked up my Bible and opened it to read and help pass the time away. I did not have another book or I am sure I would have read it instead.

I had the Living Bible and it fell open to the Psalms. I tell you the truth. I lie not! I looked on page 485 and saw these words: "And look! See the ships! And over there, the whale you made to play in the sea. Every one of these depends on you to give them daily food. You supply it, and they gather it. You open wide your hand to feed them and they are satisfied with all your bountiful provision." That is Psalm 104 verses 26-28.

We were flying low over the beautiful South China Sea. I looked out of my window and just below, close enough for me to see were two ships. I could not believe my eyes. It was as though God was speaking to me saying, "Look out the window!" I watched those two ships slowly making their way to their destined port. I realized that in that sea were thousands of fish. God was providing for them and they were satisfied.

Here I sat, wishing I were dead. I have had more "things" than most people have even heard about. I have been loved and treated kindly by my family and my friends. I have traveled and seen the world. And, I have opportunity to share my faith. I have the unbelievable privilege of knowing the God of all Creation!

I prayed, "Oh, Lord, when will I learn? Forgive me for my impatience, my anger and my hostility. Cause my love to increase and abound toward all men. Put a song in my heart and give me a thankful spirit."

God had done it again! He had showed me myself. My eyes were beginning to be open to what I looked like to Him. My vision was improving.

I know now that God had to shear away my homeland, my family members and friends in order for me to see my own heart. I was blind and He wanted me to see! God doesn't open our eyes to all our problems at once. It would be too hard for us. He continues to increase our vision as we give Him the freedom to do so.

Proverbs 29:18 "Where there is no vision, the people perish; but he that keepeth the law, happy is he." Perish means to waste away, to be in a state of decay, to be wasted or rendered useless. This is the state of a man who is mad, bitter, hostile, haughty, proud, selfish, discontent and filled with self pity.

Happy is the man who lets God change his heart. It is always beneficial when God shears His people. He knows what He is doing. It may seem at times that God is sitting on us clipping away and this process will never end. We must remember that God loves us and has the power to cause us to prosper through mishap or tragedy. We easily forget this, therefore it is necessary that we have a reminder. Sheep are the best reminders I know. I must never forget that I am like one. God tells me so and He ought to know. He made me!
Like sheep, to improve our vision, we need to be sheared!

Sheep Need Full-Time Supervision Because They Are Defenseless!

Characteristics of Sheep

When the enemy attacks, sheep are unable to defend themselves. They are not swift runners. Their bite is harmless. Most have no horns! This leaves them as easy prey. Many of their predators pass them by unless they are real hungry. It seems they want the challenge of a fight to work up an appetite!

A Shepherd's Care

The shepherd carries a rod to ward off predators. An experienced shepherd is aware that his sheep are unable to defend themselves. He knows they can't find food, they won't drink water, they fall and can't get up. They need to be sheared and they have a tendency to go astray.

ANOTHER REASON FOR THE SHEPHERD TO HONOR HIS COMMITMENT AND PROVIDE FULL-TIME SUPERVISION FOR THE SHEEP!

Characteristics of People

As a freshman in college it was glamorous (I thought) to pile onto a bed full of girls in a smoked filled dormitory room and light up a cigarette! It seemed that all the neat, popular girls smoked.

I remember my first cigarette and my last one. When I inhaled the smoke from my first drag of a Camel, I felt that I was going to faint! The girls in the room with me became distant and I could hardly hear their voices. This only lasted for a few minutes. I was determined to try another drag. I was going to learn to smoke!

The second drag was not so bad. Each one got easier and affected me less and less. I loved smoking. Nothing better than a cup of coffee and a cigarette!

I was up to about one pack a day when the word got out that these cigarettes might be dangerous. They were enemies of the human lungs.

My dad died with lung cancer at age 60 and my brother who is a surgeon told me his cancer was caused by smoking. After the funeral we went to mother's and I lit a cigarette. I will never forget my brother looking at me and saying, "How can you do that after what we have been through with dad?"

I put that cigarette out and determined to smoke no more. It did not take long for me to realize that it was going to take more than determination to get this habit out of my system.

I struggled for years trying to stop smoking. I did everything I knew to do. I found the habit more than I could handle. During my struggle I became a Christian. A friend suggested that I pray about this problem. She suggested that I ask God to give me the strength to stop smoking. I thought God had more important things to do than help me with smoking. She reminded me that I am a child of God and just as human parents are concerned for the needs of their children, God is concerned about every part of our being.

This made sense to me so I prayed and asked God to give me the strength to stop smoking. Nothing happened. I kept yielding to the desire for the cigarette and wondering why God was not helping me. I called my friend to discuss the matter. She pointed out that God was not going to come down from heaven and remove the cigarette from my lips or take it from my hand. I had to decide to give it up. I had to decide to stop smoking and go through the hard times of wanting to smoke. It would not be easy but when I turned from the desire, I would find strength from the Lord. I asked God to take away the desire. One day as I struck a match and lifted it toward my face to light a cigarette, I realized that God would take away the desire to smoke, when I stopped smoking. I blew out the match, threw the cigarettes in the garbage and said, "Lord, I will quit smoking. Now you give me the strength I am going to need to get over wanting the nicotine."

That was not the last time I wanted a cigarette. It was the last time I smoked. As I refused to yield to the desire, I began to experience the power of God in my life. I noticed that soon the desire was slipping away from me. God was working in my life, guiding me, being my Shepherd.

I realize that you can stop smoking without God. Thousands have done it. I just happened to be one who could not.

Smoking is certainly not the worst enemy man encounters. There are too many to list. Smoking just happens to be one enemy that has the possibility of eating you alive (with cancer).

Ulcer hour remedy

Alcohol is another enemy. I had to fight that one too. This one I fought without God. I managed to conquer it alone. When my three children were under three years of age, 4 p.m. to 6 p.m. were ulcer hours. Sam seldom came home before 6 o'clock.

I found that if I had a drink about 4 o'clock I calmed down. If I had another one about 4:30 I was even calmer. When I added one a half-hour later I played with the children! Drinking helped me through the nerve racking hours of the late afternoon.

One afternoon I was sitting in the yard with a neighbor. The children were playing quietly in the sandbox. The neighbor and I were drinking vodka. Time came to go home and prepare dinner. I got up and started walking home. I couldn't find the house. I kept looking and soon it came by. I started for the front door. My children were following me saying, "Mama, what is the matter with you?" I was drunk! Never in my life had I been so horrified. I was not raised to be a drunk. My parents taught me better, and my husband certainly deserved better than this.

I went straight to my bed, crawled under the cover, pulled it over my head and cried. When Sam came home I told him I had the flu! I was ashamed. I did not want Sam to know I was drunk.

That day I determined never to allow this to happen again. I was not a Christian but I knew this road led to a dead end. I don't know why I could give up alcohol and not cigarettes but that is the way it was.

The strong sex drive can be an enemy. God created us with this drive. He told us sex was meant for marriage. We are warned about having multiple sex partners. This is a cause of the spread of venereal diseases. We know that these diseases are enemies of the human body. In order to prevent the spread of these diseases we should not engage in sexual activities outside the bonds of marriage.

It would be stupid to say we should not desire to have sex but who ever said we should have everything we want? We need a shepherd who will protect us from our enemies. One who will give us the strength we need when we decide to turn from the things that are harmful to our body.

We have many more enemies. Lying, deceit, anger and bitterness are listed in the Bible as works of the flesh. I consider the flesh to be our greatest enemy. The flesh is our fallen nature. It is in us and with us 24 hours each day!

Damaging deceit

I asked Dr. Brandt what he considered to be the most serious marriage problem today. I was shocked at his answer. He quickly said "deceit". Deceit is a dangerous, deadly enemy. It is one that is hard to fight. It causes serious problems with man's mental health. A person can be a fake for so long that he really has a hard time deciding who he is. You can push your real feelings so far inside of you that you can't find them.

Being deceitful means you say one thing and believe another or you act a certain way and feel just the opposite.

I met a friend from college days. I never did like this girl. I did not like the way she wore her hair and I hated her laugh. I remember closing the door of my dormitory room when I heard her in the hall. I did not want her coming in my room to visit me.

Years after graduating I saw this girl in the grocery store. I could not avoid speaking to her. I said, "Hello it is good to see you. How have you been?" After our conversation I invited her to come to see me. We parted company and I finished my shopping. I remember walking out of the store and seeing a reflection of myself in the window.

I looked at that reflection and felt sick. I even said to myself, "You make me sick!" I got in the car and drove home. I wished I could hide. I am not sure I knew what was wrong with me. I felt dirty.

I was sick of being nice to my friends and screaming at my children. I was sick of talking so nicely on the telephone and being so nasty to my family.

My behavior caused me mental anguish. One afternoon the telephone rang. I ran to answer it and saw my children spreading mud on the windows of my house. I could not believe they were doing this. I screamed as loud as I could for them to get away from the window. I picked up the phone and as nice and sweet as possible, I said, "Hello"!

I felt like a plate glass window that someone had just thrown a brick through. I was shattered on the inside. I wanted the floor to open so I could drop out of sight. My deceit was killing me. I wanted my friends to think I was a nice, sweet, charming lady. My family saw that I was a raging tyrant.

Being deceitful was a big enemy to me. I needed a defense. I needed a Shepherd to care for me and lead me to safety. I wanted to be honest. I wanted to be real. I hated having to change the look on my face, the tone of my voice and the subject of my conversation when someone outside the family walked into my life.

The Shepherd's Care

We are told in the Bible that we have three enemies. The world, the flesh and the devil. We are constantly tempted by the world. We desire to be popular and to have the desires of our heart. Some men and women want power or position. Nothing wrong with popularity, things, power or position. It is a matter of priority. We need to care more what God thinks of us than man. When this is our attitude, God takes care of our enemies. Proverbs 16:7 "When a man's ways please the LORD, he maketh even his enemies to be at peace with him."

We should delight ourselves in (obey) God and He will give us the desires of our heart. Psalm 37:4. Trust God with your powers and positions in life. Matthew 23:12 "And whosoever shall exalt himself shall be abased; and he that shall humble himself shall be exalted."

In Ephesians chapter 6 we are told about another enemy, the devil. He is the ruler of darkness, strong and full of tricks. God tells us that we need to put on our armor so that we will be able to stand against him. We are told to use every piece of the armor to resist when he attacks.

We need the breastplate of righteousness. (We make a decision to do what is right.) We need our feet shod with the gospel of peace. (We are peace makers!) Our shield is of faith. (Faith goes before us to protect us.) Our helmet must be of salvation. (We need to know for sure that we are saved.) Our sword is the Word of God. (We must know how to use Bible verses to defend us in the face of our enemies.) Finally, we need to pray. (We should talk to God about everything.)

Winning against Satan is accomplished by the decisions we make. We decide if we want to have on the armor. We fight the daily battles trusting God to lead us, give us wisdom and strength and to keep us standing when it is all over.

Like sheep, man is defenseless and needs a Shepherd!

Sheep Need Full-Time Supervision Because They Need His Daily Touch!

Characteristics of Sheep

Sheep will come to the shepherd daily and rub against his legs or wait for a pat on the head. Once he has had a bit of personal attention from the shepherd, the sheep leaves satisfied for the day. Satisfied sheep eat, drink, get fat and grow wool. They fulfill the purpose for which they were created.

A Shepherd's Care

Prospering shepherds are those with satisfied sheep. The shepherd must make himself available to the sheep. He must reach out to them. The touch of the shepherd satisfies the sheep. An experienced shepherd desires satisfaction for his flock and through himself meets this need.

ANOTHER REASON FOR THE SHEPHERD TO HONOR HIS COMMITMENT AND PROVIDE FULL-TIME SUPERVISION FOR THE SHEEP!

Characteristics of People

We are told in the Bible that we are to live by faith. Faith comes by hearing and hearing by the Word of God. (Romans 10:17) Another word for faith is confidence. The more confidence you have in Him, the more comfortable you will be as He leads you.

Since we were designed to be led and confidence is the key motivating factor, daily contact is imperative!

Men, like sheep were created to have a need of daily contact with The Shepherd!

I have never been able to designate a certain time each day for my prayer and Bible study. Something always seemed to come up and interfere. I was frustrated and at times even angry that I had been interrupted.

I planned to pray and read my Bible daily so I looked for a time. I remember when my children were in school and I was driving in a car pool, I could enjoy Bible study waiting in the lines at the school. There were no telephones, no dishes to wash, no clothes waiting to be folded and put away. I always took my Bible on the days I picked up the children. This was truly a quiet time for me.

The Shepherd's Care

I don't mean to imply that a quiet time is the only contact you have with The Shepherd. If you have committed yourself to Him for full-time supervision, He is with you continuously.

PART II

All We Like Sheep Have Gone Astray, We Have Turned Everyone To His Own Way . . .

Having studied the first part of Isaiah 53:6, let's look at the second part: "All we like sheep have gone astray; *we have turned every one to his own way;* and the LORD hath laid on him the iniquity of us all."

It is our nature to want our own way. This is a natural tendency for all of us. We get involved in obtaining what we want and it is possible for us to forget everything else except reaching our goal.

When sheep find pasture, their only interest is eating. Their main concern is the next blade of grass. It is easy to stray as they nibble away with their eye on the grass instead of the shepherd.

Since the sheep don't watch the shepherd, the shepherd must watch the sheep. He walks among them as they eat and makes sure they stay near him. If just one little lamb strays from the fold, the shepherd goes to bring him back. We, like sheep have a strong tendency to become preoccupied with satisfying our own desires and we easily wonder away from The Shepherd. This strong tendency was first manifested in the garden of Eden.

When God formed the universe, He put the stars in place, the sun began to shine and the trees stood tall. The green grass grew and the birds flew in the air and the fish swam in the sea. When the cattle roamed over the earth and creeping things crept around, God created Adam and Eve.

The LORD God planted a garden eastward in Eden. In this garden there were only trees pleasant to the sight. All the food was good to eat. The tree of the knowledge of good and evil was planted there.

God brought Adam to this garden and said, "Enjoy the garden. You may freely eat of it all except the fruit from the tree of the knowledge of good and evil. Do not eat from this tree. If you do you will surely die!"

God decided man should not live alone so He put Adam to sleep and from his side made Eve. They were in the garden with everything good and desirable. God told them specifically what not to do. There was a serpent in this garden and he was a subtle creature. He approached Eve and questioned the Word of God. Did God say you could eat the fruit of the trees of the garden?

I love Eve's answer. She said, "God said we can eat all the fruit from all the trees except the one in the midst of the garden. God said we can not eat this fruit neither can we touch it or we will die."

I can't find where God said anything about touching the fruit. Eve added to the story. I find myself doing this. I love to add to the story to make it more effective!

The serpent said to Eve, "You won't die. God knows that if you eat from the tree of the knowledge of good and evil, you will be as a god!"

Eve listened to the wrong voice. She knew full well that God said she was not to eat from this tree. She looked at the fruit as she listened to the voice of the serpent. It was pleasant to the eye. It was desirable.

Eve, looked at and desired that which God had told her she could not have. Listening to the voice of the serpent and believing him, she reached out and took the forbidden fruit. Eve had walked with God and heard the Word of God — personally. When the test came she chose to have her own way. This powerful tendency overruled her knowledge of God and His Word.

Eve ate the fruit and then took it to Adam. What a human thing to do. Misery loves company! Eve knew the Word of God but she simply did what she wanted to. Like a sheep Eve went her own way. This was the entrance of sin into the human race. We are all born with this natural tendency. We don't have to learn this type behavior. "Behold, I was shapen in iniquity; and in sin did my mother conceive me." (Psalm 51:5). The word iniquity is used to described our tendency to want our own way.

I have had the opportunity to raise three children. Now I am observing my three grandsons. It is more fun to watch grandchildren. They go home at night! (This is why they are called grand!)

Having observed two generations of children, adds to my confidence that we are born wanting to have our own way!

Playpen drama

Sam was 18 months old when Dawn was born. Soon she was old enough to play in his playpen with him. We looked forward to the day they would play together.

That big day arrived. Daddy Sam got the camera. I dressed the children for the picture. We placed the toys in the pen and put Sam in first. When he realized Dawn was about to join him, he started gathering all the toys and placing them in the corner. With both arms outstretched, feet apart, he made a bold stand to defend his toys.

We sat Dawn in the opposite corner. She spotted a toy and went for it! Sam started to scream. Then he hit Dawn's arm as she reached for the toy. She joined him in screaming.

In shock, we looked at each other. What had we raised? How did Sam get to be selfish? Then we realized that even an 18-month-old is like a sheep.

Lamb learns early

Mark is the oldest grandchild. When he was three months old, Dawn and Curry asked us to keep him. They wanted to go to dinner and a movie. Sam and I were eating dinner and Mark was sitting on the floor in his little seat. I heard him make a strange noise. It sounded as if he was choking. Naturally, I jumped up to check on him.

Here was this three-month-old baby faking a cry. He would struggle and strain to cry and then look at me to see if I would take him out of his seat.

I said to Sam, "Look at this baby. He has already learned that when he cries his grandma comes running. He is already working me. What a smart grandchild I have."

I taught Dawn all the stories about sheep and I told her that each wants his own way. She loved the stories and told me that she believed them. When her little Mark was two years old, I received a telephone call from a desperate daughter. She was crying because little Mark was throwing his first temper tantrum. I could hear him screaming in the background. I thought he must have been seriously injured. Dawn said he wanted to spread the peanut butter on his bread. She spread it for him.

Mark fell to the floor screaming as if he were in excruciating pain! He kicked and cried and beat his head on the floor. All this because he could not spread the peanut butter on the bread!

Dawn was hysterical. She said, "Mother, what am I going to do. I have never seen him act this way before. Do you think something is terribly wrong with him?"

I told Dawn to quietly and calmly pick him up and tell him that this behavior was not acceptable. (I did not think she would do it, but she did.)

She called me several hours later. She was laughing as she told me that she had picked Mark up as he kicked and screamed. She quietly told him to "stop screaming." She said, "Mom, he did what I told him to do. He stopped screaming and he ate his sandwich.

Mark doesn't fall on the floor and kick any more. He learned at an early age that kicking and screaming did not get him what he wanted. He tries other tricks and will continue to do so but at least he is quieter.

God has given each of us different personalities and different ways of expressing ourselves. Even with these differences we find we have one thing in common. We, like sheep, want our own way!

Contrasts

Sam, my husband, is a quiet, consistent, stubborn, bullheaded man who wants his way. As of this writing, I have been married to Sam for 32 years. I remember only one time seeing him really lose his temper.

I am loud, expressive, quick to change my mind, stubborn, bullheaded and want my own way. I used to pride myself on the fact that Sam always knew where he stood with me. I told him!

Sam prided himself on the fact that when he got upset with me, I never knew it. He thought he was being loving, kind and tactful as he covered up his feelings. For years I thought he was good and I was bad.

For years I wished Sam would speak up and he wished I would shut up. We had no communication, I thought! The problem was that we did not talk about what I wanted to talk about. Sam hates to have a confrontation. He doesn't like for us to have a problem. When we do, his philosophy is to ignore it and hope it will go away.

When problems arise I like to discuss them at least 16 times! I want to resolve them over days of discussion.

Sam and I had to learn that we are like sheep wanting to have our own way. We discovered that we will want our way as long as we live. This is not intended to be demeaning or pessimistic but is to motivate us to see the need for full-time supervision.

We had to learn to cooperate. When Sam and I have a difference of opinion, we must find a common meeting ground. There are times one must yield totally to the other. At other times we compromise. You can't yield or compromise when you enter a meeting demanding to have your way.

We both had to change. Sam had to learn that there were times when unpleasant subjects needed to be discussed. I had to learn to say something one time and know that Sam heard me. We learn how to enter into a conversation from a study of Philippians chapter 2, verse 3: "Let nothing be done through strife or vainglory; but in lowliness of mind let each esteem other better than themselves."

This is the Word of God on how to work together. Ignore what God says and you will suffer. Listen, take heed and you will prosper.

God tells us there is a time to do nothing. I find this to be the hardest thing I have to do. When I want something, I hate to do nothing about getting it. He says when there is strife (contention, fighting, quarreling) don't do anything. When there is vainglory or self seeking, (when things had better turn out your way) don't do anything. Wait.

We are told to wait until we can think more highly of the other person than we do of ourselves.

Because we continue to be like sheep as long as we live, we will always want to have our way. We should not feel badly about ourselves when we find that we always want it to go our way. We need to pay careful attention to our reaction when we don't get it. Anger is man's most common reaction. Both secular and Christian counselors agree that it is one of the most harmful reactions we experience. That being so, I have always been puzzled as to why man is so defensive about giving up anger.

Several years ago, the puzzle was solved. After spending many years in counseling, I understand that anger is man's best tool for getting his way. You get mad enough and yell loud enough or pout for several days and people usually give in and let you have what you want. What a threat to give up our most effective tool!

If you display your anger people will either give you your way or get out of your way leaving you alone.

Years ago, Dr. Brandt warned me, "When a person has to always have his way, people will get out of the way. When people get out of your way, you are left alone. So if you are a person who always has to have your way, you are preparing yourself for a life of loneliness!"

Israel's King David

When kings went forth into battle, David was home sacked out! He got out of bed in the late afternoon. To shake off his drowsiness, he went to the rooftop for some fresh air. David saw a woman taking her bath. She was beautiful to behold and he desired to have her. As the king, David had sentenced adulterers to death by stoning.

This was the most painful means of execution. David knew full well what would happen if he committed adultery with Bathsheba. He did it anyway! Sending for her, David slept with her. She conceived and when David found out, he knew he was in trouble!

Bathsheba's husband Uriah was at war. David had to find a way out of his dilemma. He sent for Uriah to come spend a few nights with his wife.

Uriah came but he could not bear to think of his comrades in arms suffering on the battlefield while he was comfortable in the arms of his wife. He slept outside the door of David's house. Despite David's repeated efforts, Uriah refused to sleep with Bathsheba!

David's plan was foiled. He sent orders to Uriah's captain to place him on the front line of battle.

Uriah was killed. David married Bathsheba and she had the child. The prophet Nathan informed David the child would die because of David's adultery and murder.

David was selected by God to be king over Israel. He was familiar with the laws of God. His strong desire to have his way caused Him to put aside his sense of right and wrong. His strong natural tendency to have his way overruled:

his knowledge of the law of God
his commitment to his God
his fear of the penalty of the law of God
his reputation (this is the man of whom it was said — a man after the heart of God)
his commitment to his country
his conscience
his personal concern for Bathsheba and her husband
his desire to remain in power
the preservation of his emotional stability.

David paid a price for his actions. In the 32nd Psalm, he described his suffering from the sins of adultery and murder. He said his bones waxed old, his head roared, the hand of God was heavy upon him day and night, there was a dryness to his physical and spiritual being.

This condition resulted from David keeping his silence — his not confessing his sin to the Lord.

In verse 5 David gives us a clear and thorough example to follow: He said:
1. he acknowledged his sin against God
2. he confessed his transgression against the law of God
3. he did not hide his iniquity — the root cause of both his sin and his transgression. The proof of which was born in David's words, "Thou forgave the iniquity of my sin."

David says there was something behind his sin and it is called iniquity. We, like sheep have gone astray, we have turned every one to his own way. We like sheep need a shepherd to guide us and direct our paths in the way of righteousness for the Lord's sake.

PART III

All We Like Sheep Have Gone Astray; Each Has Turned To His Own Way; *And The Lord Has Laid On Him The Iniquity Of Us All.*

We have seen how we are like sheep. We understand the strong tendency to want our way. Now we need to see the provisions God has made on our behalf.

The word LORD in this verse refers to God. The word Him refers to Jesus Christ. This is a prophetic verse. When Isaiah wrote, the Messiah had not come.

Jesus Christ, the Messiah, came into the world so that the Father could lay on Him one thing common to us all. This one thing is selfishness. Not all men are adulterers. Not all men are murderers. Some people go through life and never steal but all are selfish and want to have their own way.

When we are born, we inherit the nature of Adam. We have seen how he and Eve acted selfishly, went against the word of God and ate the forbidden fruit. After all, this did not seem to be such a terrible thing to do. There was no one around so no one seemed to be hurt. They simply listened to the wrong voice and went their own way. The serpent tempted them to do what they wanted to do rather than what God told them to do!

Upon eating the fruit, Adam and Eve immediately felt guilty. They were in this wonderful spot, the garden spot of the universe. They had been naked all their lives and were comfortable. Now they were ashamed. They sewed fig leaves together and made an apron for a covering. In the cool of the day, God walked in the garden. He called for Adam and found him hiding, afraid of the loving God. God asked Adam if he had eaten the forbidden fruit. Adam quickly told God that he ate it because of the woman He had given to be with him. Turning to Eve, God asked her about what had happened. She quickly told God it was because of the serpent. Adam and Eve did not want to accept the responsibility for their behavior.

God cursed the serpent, multiplied the sorrow of Eve in childbirth and told Adam that in the sweat of his brow he would provide for his family. In other words, the serpent would pay for what he had done by crawling on his belly, the woman would suffer in childbirth and the man would work hard to provide for his family. In Galatians 6:7 Paul writes, "Be not deceived; God is not mocked; for whatsoever a man soweth, that shall he also reap." We pay for what we do!

Now comes the Good News! After informing Adam and Eve of the consequences of their behavior, He, The LORD GOD, made coats of skins and clothed them! The fig leaves that Adam and Eve had hoped would hid their sin, failed to do so. This covering represents the work of Adam and Eve. This was their means of covering their guilt. Fig leaves symbolize man's works as he attempts to cover his guilt and satisfy God. Man's works would not satisfy God so He killed an animal, took the skins and covered His children. This is a picture of the substitutionary atoning death of Jesus Christ which would provide for man's sin and guilt. The shedding of blood represents the giving of life. This was God's way of showing that he would provide the life to cover the sin of man.

God provided the life through the person of Jesus Christ. He was the GOD Man.

He rode a donkey into Jerusalem and gave himself to be crucified. Man did not come after Jesus to arrest Him. God presented Himself to man just as He had in the garden of Eden. When He was nailed to the cross he cried out to God, "Why hast thou forsaken me?" It was at this moment in time that God poured on Jesus "the iniquity" of us all.

God turned away from His only begotten Son because He is holy and cannot look upon sin. The Bible doesn't record that man killed Jesus. He voluntarily gave His life for us. It tells us in Matthew chapter 27 verse 50 that Jesus cried again with a loud voice and gave up the ghost.

Jesus gave his life for His sheep! No man had the power to take life from the Living God. God teaches us that the wages of sin is death. (Roman 6:23) When we sin, we get paid! Our payment is death.

The gospel is called The Good News. There is no better news than the news that God died in our place. It is hard to believe that God, The Creator and Sustainer of the universe would become a man and take our place in death so that we might be free of sin and have eternal life!

The covering of Adam and Eve is a picture of what God will do for mankind. Jesus' sacrifice is the only sacrifice for sin acceptable to God.

Man's responsibility is to reach out and accept it. Adam and Eve could have refused to accept God's provision.

One of the most difficult things for man to do is accept a gift. He is afraid he will be obligated to the giver or that the giver will require something undesirable of him.

Red jacket — red faces

We were in California with some wealthy friends. While Sam stayed home with Dave, Nan asked me to go shopping with her. She was busy making a purchase and I tried to stay out of her way. I saw a red jacket that was very expensive. Just for fun, I tried it on. Just as I put on the jacket Nan came to tell me she had finished shopping. She commented that she liked the jacket.

We left the store and went to meet Sam and Dave for coffee. Nan asked us to order her coffee while she ran to buy some shoes. She returned and we finished our coffee. She suggested we show Sam the jacket. On the way to the shop I told Sam how much it cost and he should not get excited over it even if he liked it. He assured me he would not!

When we entered the store Nan asked me to show Sam the jacket. She had something to show Dave!

The jacket was gone. It had been sold. Just 30 minutes ago it hung there but now it was gone! The sales lady came from the back room with a package. She said, "Are you Mrs. Peeples?" I said, "Yes, I am." She said, "I have a jacket for you and the ticket is marked paid."

Sam started lecturing me. He said, "Why did you tell Nan you liked the jacket?" I said, "I did not tell her I liked the jacket, she told *me* she liked the jacket!" Sam said, "You did tell her or she would not have bought you something you didn't like!" I said, "I did not tell her!" He said, "I am embarrassed, I can not let you accept this gift. It is too much money for them to spend!" I said, "Well, what do you suggest I do about it!"

As you can imagine, with each sentence our voices grew louder and our striving became evident. When I realized how loud we were speaking, I looked to see if Nan and Dave could hear us.

Dave is about 6 feet 4 inches tall. It was not hard to find them in a crowded department store! I saw them over in the corner smiling as they watched me receive the gift they had so graciously offered!

I could tell by their expressions that they were excited over being able to give me this jacket. They, the smiling givers, stood in the corner getting great pleasure in doing this, while we, the receivers quarreled in the opposite corner.

Turning to Sam I said, "Look at the gleam in their eyes and the smile on their faces." They want to do this for us. We must let them. We must take this gift!

He agreed. We walked over to Nan and Dave and simply said, "Thank you!" It was hard to put away our pride but it was the correct thing to do.

I still enjoy my red jacket because of its beauty but each time I wear it, I appreciate more what I learned through receiving it. I had to put away my pride in order to accept the jacket. In the same way, I must put away my pride to accept God's gift of salvation. The blood of Jesus Christ was shed on the cross to take away my sin. This is the only provision ever made to take away sin. By faith I accept His great gift of love and thank Him for it.

When I asked Jesus Christ to come into my life, I became a child of God. He became my Shepherd. I can trust Him to provide for me, to comfort me, to give me an abundant life on earth plus life with Him in heaven when I die.

Many people struggle over the need for a Savior. They don't see themselves as sinners. Comparing themselves with others, they see themselves as good. "For we dare not make ourselves of the number, or compare ourselves with some that commend themselves; but they measuring themselves by themselves, and comparing themselves among themselves, are not wise." (II Corinthians 10:12) We are sinners because of our selfish iniquitous nature.

Have you ever made the decision to accept God's provision for your sin? If not, you could do so right now. This is done through a simple act of faith. Pray and ask Christ to come into your life as your personal Savior and Lord. Ask Him to forgive you of your sins and to take control of your life.

Assurance

When you invite Christ into your life, you can rest assured that He will come in. He said in Revelations 3:20, "Behold, I stand at the door, and knock; if any man hear my voice, and open the door, I will come in to him, and will sup with him, and he with me."

Once Christ comes into your life, he never leaves you. In Hebrews 13:5b He says, "I will never leave thee, nor forsake thee." In Romans 8:38-39, "For I am persuaded, that neither death, not life, nor angels, nor principalities, nor powers nor things present, nor things to come, Nor height, nor depth, nor any other creature, shall be able to separate us from the love of God, which is in Christ Jesus our Lord."

You can relax, be comfortable and know that now you have a Shepherd who desires to care for and lead you and has all the necessary resources for doing the job and doing it well!

It is critical that we know that wanting our own way, iniquity, is the source of our sins. An understanding of the word iniquity teaches us that we must deal with the source.

The word "iniquity" appears as a singular noun in Isaiah 53:6 and most other places where it is used. When lists of sins are found in the Bible, the plural use of the word sin is used.

Conclusion: Sins, plural, have as their singular source, iniquity.

The word iniquity is defined in Isaiah 53:6. "All we like sheep have gone astray, each has turned to his own way and the Lord hath laid on Him the iniquity of us all." Iniquity means turning to or having to have your own way.

God took upon Him the iniquity (source) and the sins (result) of the world. You will find these two words mentioned together in many places in the Psalms. The fact that they are mentioned together but separate demonstrates that they are not the same.

Remember King David?

In the time of year when kings went forth to battle, David tarried in Jerusalem. He slept during the day and when he awoke in the afternoon, he went to the roof and saw Bathsheba bathing. He sent his servants for her. His iniquity was wanting to have his way with her and his sin was adultery.

Bathsheba got pregnant. David was in trouble. He ordered Uriah, Bathsheba's husband, home from battle. David wanted them to sleep together. This would provide a cover for his sin. He told Uriah that he should come home for rest. Now David's sin was deceit.

Uriah refused to sleep with his wife. David's cover had failed. He had to devise another method for covering his sin. He did this by ordering Uriah into the front lines of battle. A few days later Uriah was killed. Now David's sin was murder.

In Psalm 32 David writes about the breakdown of his spiritual, emotional, mental and physical condition. As you read through this Psalm you find the reasons for these breakdowns:

Verse 3: "When I kept silence, my bones waxed old through my roaring all the day long." David's silence refers to the fact that he did not confess his sins. Because of this he experienced many physical symptoms. David felt old and his bones ached. I have always wondered if he developed arthritis! His head roared and he could not stop the sound of the roaring. Could this be a migraine headache?

In verse 4: "For day and night thy hand was heavy upon me: my moisture is turned into the drought of summer. Selah." David experienced this heaviness because of his continued delay in confessing his sin. Now more symptoms are developing. David felt a dryness in his soul. Next the word selah is used. Selah means to pause and think on this. The word is always used to emphasize the previous statement.

Verse 5: "I acknowledged my sin unto thee, and mine iniquity have I not hid. I said, I will confess my transgressions unto the LORD: and thou forgavest the iniquity of my sin. Selah." David stopped hiding from God. David agreed with God concerning his sins. He did not hide from God the fact that he did what he did because he wanted to. Notice the word selah appears again. He confessed to God that he had broken God's laws. Confess means to agree with God. It literally means to say the same thing God says. David was no longer making excuses for his behavior. He was saying, "God, I did it and I agree with you that it was wrong." You said, "Thou shalt not commit adultery, nor murder and thou shalt not deceive." "I broke your law."

David provides an example of how we should come before God and thoroughly deal with our sin. He had sinned against God. He had transgressed the law of God. He also dealt with his iniquity which was the reason for both his sin and transgression.

Verse 6, "For this shall every one that is godly pray unto thee in a time when thou mayest be found: surely in the floods of great waters they shall not come nigh unto him." Due to David's long period of suffering, he is advising us to confess our sins as quickly as possible. The presence of unconfessed sin causes a person to lose confidence in God. If unconfessed sins are allowed to accumulate it is like waters rising in a flood. The rising waters seem to distance us from God.

Verse 7, "Thou art my hiding place; Thou dost preserve me from trouble; Thou dost surround me with songs of deliverance." This sounds like a different person. Now David says that God is his hiding place. He states that God will preserve him from trouble and compass him about with songs of deliverance. God is again leading David as his Shepherd. God will lead David in the paths of righteousness for His namesake. God will lead David beside the still waters where his thirst will be satisfied. God will lead David to the green pastures.

Verse 8, "I will instruct thee and teach thee in the way which thou shalt go: I will guide thee with mine eyes." David has been speaking. Now God speaks and promises instruction and guidance. It is important to take note of the steps David took to get instruction and guidance from God!

Verse 9, "Be ye not as the horse, or as the mule, which have no understanding; whose mouth must be held in with bit and bridle, lest they come near unto thee." David warns us not to be stubborn as a mule. We should not let pride keep us from accepting God's gift of love and his provision for forgiveness. The picture here is of a mule having to be driven. We have said earlier that we are like sheep. Sheep are meant to be led, not driven.

Verse 10, "Many sorrows shall be to the wicked; but he that trusteth in the LORD, mercy shall compass him about." David speaks from experience because of the sorrow he experienced from his wickedness. When he turned back to the Lord, he experienced His mercy. Mercy means God's grace in action.

Verse 11, "Be glad in the LORD, and rejoice, ye righteous: and shout for joy, all ye that are upright in heart." David is able to rejoice and shout for joy. He has chosen to do what is right and now has a clean heart! He feels good!

A surprised father

Iniquity means I want to have my own way. We see what happened to David because of it. We can look at children and see it manifest. They learn at an early age to cry and get what they want. Their crying turns into temper tantrums. These tantrums work even better.

An evangelist friend in India told us of his concern for his daughter's temper tantrums. He often went on evangelistic trips for weeks at the time. When he returned to his city, he went home to speak to his family and leave his luggage. Then he went to the office to take care of his mail. His intentions were to hurry to the office, complete his work and return to his family.

Paul said each time he arrived home Stephanie cried and had a temper tantrum when he started for the office. He tried to explain that he would return soon and spend time with her. This did not help Stephanie. After several years of this behavior, Paul was uncertain what to do.

On these occasions Stephanie tightly grasped her father's leg. Paul said when he screamed loudly, she turned him loose. He was convicted about his screaming but realized this was the only way to escape Stephanie's grasp.

We laughed at Paul as we told him that he was a good teacher. Stephanie observed that when you scream, you get your way!

He was shocked when we told him where Stephanie had learned this means of getting her way.

I have seen the president of a bank have a temper tantrum. I have seen a respected surgeon have a temper tantrum. I have seen beautiful, well educated mothers have temper tantrums. These people had tantrums in my presence because something in their life had not gone their way.

Some of the things they wanted to happen were good things. When what you want is good and you don't get your way, look out! This is a dangerous place to be. You will justify your anger because your desire is good. Your desire might not only be good, it could also be God's desire.

It is a Godly thing for a man to want his child to live a moral life. When the child strays, the father believes he is justified in losing his temper. He hopes the child will change when he sees how his behavior has affected his father. What a shame to communicate to this child that his father's emotional stability is dependent on his behavior!

When an unmarried girl gets pregnant and her weeping mother goes to bed with depression, she is of little value to her daughter. The mother justifies her behavior. She hopes the daughter will realize the seriousness of the situation by the effect it has on her mother.

When a man has an affair, the wife thinks she must show her displeasure by becoming bitter and miserable. How would her husband know how this has affected her unless she provides a constant reminder!

It is difficult for us to realize that a child who has gone astray needs a kind, tender-hearted, patient mom or dad to gently but firmly lead him back to the right path. Angry parents cause children to dread coming home.

When a young unmarried girl gets pregnant, she needs a comfortable, calm loving mom and dad to help her make good decisions concerning her problem. A depressed mom makes it difficult for her to go home.

A man who is having an affair needs a comfortable loving wife who can calmly communicate to him that his behavior is not acceptable. A screaming, pouting, angry woman makes it hard for a man to come home at the end of the day.

Vengeance belongs to the Lord. Your anger and resentment don't help anybody. They usually make things worse. If you have a loved one who has gone astray you should have a desire to lead that one to The Shepherd. In order to lead them to The Shepherd, you will need to be in good spiritual condition. Benjamin Franklin once said, "He who cannot obey cannot command."

When we talk about being in good spiritual condition, we are making reference to walking in the Spirit. Many people have a variety of ideas about what it means to walk in the Spirit. God's only means of controlling our selfish nature (iniquity) is through the control of the Holy Spirit. Many Christians have tried other things but have found them powerless.

I believe the following five steps are necessary to enter into the Spirit controlled life.

1) Submit
   "I beseech you therefore, brethren, by the mercies of God, that ye present your bodies a living sacrifice, holy, acceptable unto God, which is your reasonable service."
   Roman 12:1
   If you do not start with total submission to the Lord, you don't get started.

2) Identify sin
   "And when he is come, he will reprove the world of sin, of righteousness, and of judgment:
   John 16:8

One of the major benefits of submitting your life to the Lord is the convicting work of the Holy Spirit. He will accurately identify your sins. Man needs this because his heart is deceitful.

"The heart is deceitful above all things and desperately wicked: who can know it? I the Lord search the heart, I try the reins, even to give every man according to his ways and according to the fruit of his doings.
Jeremiah 17:9 & 10

"He that covereth his sins shall not prosper: but whoso confesseth and forsaketh them shall have mercy."
Proverbs 28:13

3) Confess
"If we confess our sins, he is faithful and just to forgive us our sins, and to cleanse us from all unrighteousness."
I John 1:9

Identification of sin is for a purpose — confession.
Confession means "agreeing with God" or "calling it the same thing." Notice the two benefits, forgiveness and cleansing.

4) Be controlled
"And be not drunk with wine, wherein is excess; but be filled with the Spirit."
Ephesians 5:18

Being controlled by the Holy Spirit is not an option, it is a command!

5) Be consistent
"This I say then, Walk in the Spirit and ye shall not fulfill the lust of the flesh."
Galatians 5:16

This verse doesn't say the desire will cease, it says, you don't have to fulfill it! This promise of consistency in this verse fulfills the need in the Christian's life. When we walk in the Spirit, we know that God is leading us where He wants us to go.

In order to maintain your walk in the Spirit, it will be necessary to identify your sin, confess it and replace it with the fruit of the Spirit. As God reveals areas of your life He wants to control, be quick to yield to Him.

As I come to the end of my story, I encourage you to accept the truth that we are all like sheep. It is natural and normal for us to desire to have our own way. I have not come to a place in life where I stop wanting my way and going astray. Because of this I need a shepherd. Through my Shepherd's teaching I have learned to pay attention to my responses when things don't go my way. Especially when my way is right!

I have learned to agree with God as quickly as possible when I sin. He has been faithful to forgive and cleanse me. As I continue to follow Him, my life gets more exciting. The older I get, the better I feel. My bones don't ache and I don't feel the heaviness from depression that I have felt before. I must never forget that as long as I live I will need a shepherd. I must remember to commit each day to The Shepherd and trust Him to lead me where He would have me to go. I encourage you to commit your days to Him. Let Him take the burden from your back, provide for you and guide you to His provisions.

God bless you and keep you in His wonderful and loving care!

THE END

Psalm 23

The Lord is my shepherd; I shall not want. He maketh me to lie down in green pastures: he leadeth me beside the still waters. He restoreth my soul: he leadeth me in the paths of righteousness for his name's sake. Yea, though I walk through the valley of the shadow of death, I will fear no evil: for thou art with me; thy rod and thy staff they comfort me. Thou preparest a table before me in the presence of mine enemies: thou anointest my head with oil; my cup runneth over. Surely goodness and mercy shall follow me all the days of my life: and I will dwell in the house of the Lord for ever.

Additional Materials by this Author:

1. Book

   Parenting: An Heir Raising Experience
      Raising Your Child With Confidence $16.00
         Dr. and Mrs. Peeples

2. Book

   All We Like Sheep $14.00

3. "Be Good to Yourself"

   How to Respond Properly to Everyday Stress
      Dr. and Mrs. Peeples

   Video (VHS) Tape Series $35.00

4. *Living Above Your Circumstances*
      Dr. and Mrs. Peeples

   Cassette Tape Series (6 tapes) $38.00

5. Assorted note cards of pictures in
   All We Like Sheep Book (10) $8.00

To order send payment plus $2.50 postage to:

The Sheep Shoppe
P. O. Box 531147
Birmingham, Alabama 35253
(205) 871-0380

Alabama residents please add 8% sales tax.